YOU ARE NOT YOUR PAST

Encouraging Believers to Rise Up Out of the Ashes of Their Former Identity and Follow Jesus

ANNETTE MIRAMONTEZ

YOU ARE NOT YOUR PAST

Encouraging Believers to Rise Up Out of the Ashes of Their Former Identity and Follow Jesus

By Annette Miramontez

Published by:
LIFEWISE BOOKS
PO BOX 1072
Pinehurst, TX 77362
LifeWiseBooks.com

annettemiramontez.com
heavensent.com

Print: 978-1-952247-76-7
Ebook: 978-1-952247-77-4

DEDICATION

I would like to dedicate this book in loving memory of my beloved parents John and Adrianna Miramontez.

To my precious gems, my children:
Melissa, Kristy, Laura, Andrew, and Sofia.

To my unborn son, who I will meet at the gates of heaven.

To my great joys, my grandchildren:
Peyton and Mariyah.

To my heavenly Father, who "makes my feet like the feet of a deer; he causes me to stand on the heights"
(Psalm 18:33, NIV).

SPECIAL THANKS

To Joan Hunter Ministries, whose love and support prompted me in my journey of becoming an ordained minister and an author.

To Charity Bradshaw of LifeWise Books, who lovingly taught me and guided me to publish my first book.

To the pastor-friends I made during our ordination in April of 2019: Sue, Robbie, Theresa, Debbie, and Deborah.

CONTENTS

CHAPTER ONE

STARTING POINT

GET FOCUSED

I have lived more than half of my life span. Like many, I have endured the countless tragedies and sorrows that have molded and shaped me into who I am today. I give the glory to God for the changes in me, from glory to glory. To speak of regrets, I have none. All that has taken place was necessary and in the will of God. Today, I can speak those words with ease. Because of what I have been through—traumatic events at a young age, sexual incest, teen pregnancy, and mental health issues—I have become a strong confident Christian woman.

Unfortunately, I suffered abuse physically and emotionally. I have a story to tell from the grips of domestic violence, designed to take me to victory over my circumstances and life situations. I faced physical abuse from the hands of past lovers. I also faced abuse from my own children. I later realized they were suffering the sting of abandonment from our family's divorce. My husband at the time, the father of four of my children, left our seventeen-year marriage right before Christmas of '96. His choice to shirk the responsibility of our family of six and turn to a lifestyle of alcohol and drugs was more than I could handle at that time.

All of the shenanigans once considered as setbacks were catalysts used to propel me forward and be used in the kingdom of God. You see, I can now minister to the suffering and oppressed because I can truly say to them, "I know what you're going through," and I will know how to pray with them because I know there's a Redeemer who lives and sets the captive free.

I have been saved and delivered in every sense of those words. There is hope and a way of escape. I did not come to those terms right away. In fact, after the initial shock of losing the father of my kids and my high school sweetheart, I was not able to eat or get out of bed for two weeks. I turned to Jesus. I could then realize that God's plan for my life had not changed just because I was rejected by my first love.

God chose me to be born in my particularly large family to make a difference. I am the youngest girl. My father is a second-generation Mexican American who worked extremely hard for my family's survival. I realized all my work ethics came from him. My mother is Native American of the Coeur d'Alene tribe from Idaho, with French descendants in the blood line from the Jesuit priests known as The Black Robes. Because of the French quotient, my children are not Native American enough to be registered into the tribe. However, my children are considered descendants of an enrolled member of the Coeur d'Alene tribe of Idaho. Most of all, we are children of the Most-High God.

My parents lived on the reservation the last twenty years of their lives. I was born on the Yakima reservation and lived there in a small town in Eastern Washington for the first six years of my life. A good many of my relatives remain there, and we see them at our annual family reunion. A good many of my cousins currently work in farm labor and warehouse packing company jobs, as did my father. Those jobs are what is readily available.

I am a mother of six (one in heaven) and grandmother to a grandson and a granddaughter. I currently live in a not-so-favorable part of a small city in Pierce County in Washington state known for drug use and high crime. Nevertheless, God has promised a house for me and daughter. Despite my middle-aged body with the aches and pains and my feeble gait, I am able to work hard at my job to get where I need to be. When we desire to be blessed it requires action on our part. God will bless what we put our hands to. Providing ample shelter is in His perfect will for us.

I know I am strong in the Lord, and I am created in His image. He once spoke over me to, "Never be ashamed of what you do for a living because you're just like my son." Jesus was a carpenter. You see, I am a housekeeper. I've been doing this kind of work now for twenty years, mostly in the hospital setting. Now, I work in the clinical setting in a nearby Indian community surrounded by Native people who treat me well and like what I do. When I pass them in the hallways at the end of their shifts and the beginning of mine, we say, "Hoyt" ("goodbye" in the Puyallup Indian language) with a nod of the head and "See you later." I do have great pay and benefits. I will work here until I retire in around 2031 with a retirement plan. Glory to God, great things He has done!

In reflecting upon my life and what I've endured, more and more I do compare life to a race set before us. I feel in my head that I am the same person as when I was thirty years old with just more wisdom. But then when I look in the mirror and see the gray hairs and the jowls, I do concur I am a middle-aged woman. With aging, I do like to remember what it was like to be young. My mind often travels back in time at different ages, like when I was twelve years old and very athletic. I had joined the girls track and field team. I vividly recall working so hard and running every day as part of my training to prepare for a big competition. I wanted to win so badly that it was all I could think about. My mother even bought me my first pair of red, white, and blue Nikes.

Clad in my running jersey and pin-striped shorts, I was prepared to run in the all-state girls track and field event. I was to do my part in the baton relay as the third-leg runner. The piercing gun fired loudly, the crowd erupted in excitement, and I was startled, but then the girls at the starting line thrust forward in a race to win.

The long-legged, tall girls in the opposing track teams began to intimidate me, as fear called out from the sidelines. Each girl ran in her own lane, gaining momentum. The first-leg runner passed the baton to our second-leg runner alongside the others, and she took off. They quickly came into view, and I could plainly see the pure competitive determination on each one's countenance. I began to feel the effects of adrenaline running through my veins as I anticipated my turn.

Finally, my teammate was quickly approaching, so I began a light jog. She seemed scared and tired as I looked over my shoulder at her. She passed the baton to me, and I quickly took off. In that moment, I remembered what my mother said to me earlier that day: "Run like a deer." I instantly shot forth like a rocket and ran like crazy, passing up the girls on both sides of me. I could hear my coach yelling, "Go, Annette!"

I became aware that my parents were in the stands, which kept me running to pass on the baton to the fourth-leg runner, who bought us to the finish line. This tremendous event was something I trained a lot for. Our efforts paid off well that day. We won fourth place, and I won some other ribbons in the individual events. I remember the proud look on my dad's face. He was so excited with a smile, and I shall never forget it.

Sometimes when running the race of life, we do grow weary when the cheers from the sidelines diminish, and all we can hear are taunts of fear, such as, "This is getting too hard. You cannot do this. You are too tired. Just stop and rest." In our exhaustion, we must rise up and stay strong. Even when we are so tired, what we must consider is what fear is and who belongs to the voices we are listening to. God's Word says we have an adversary.

> *"Be alert and of sober mind. Your enemy, the devil prowls around like a lion looking for someone to devour." (1 Peter 5:8, NIV)*

The enemy of our souls is on the sidelines waiting and watching for whom he can seize upon. If you have ever watched any wildlife videos of lions and their tactics to hunt for food, you would see that they wait on the sidelines following herds of running prey. They notice when an animal is weak or falls away from the rest of the herd where they are more vulnerable to attack. Satan and his legions of demons are similar, as they wait on the sidelines waiting for us to become weary and weak for the perfect opportunity to attack. In order to be alert and sober-minded, we need to look to God for strength. From personal experience, I believe this comes from communing with God daily in prayer and time reading His Word. After leaving church services, I often feel refreshed and strengthened.

I was born into a large Catholic family. I have five brothers and three sisters. I am the youngest sister. My parents brought us up attending church regularly every Sunday. My Native American mother was raised in an all-girls Catholic boarding school. Unlike other boarding school experiences for Indian children, my mom's experience was not a bad one. Her grandfather was the last chief of the Coeur d'Alene tribe, Andrew Seltice (my son is named after him). For this reason, I believe that is why she was treated well.

These Catholic nuns raised my mother well with training in classical piano and with a standard that everything in your surroundings should be clean and orderly. Mother wanted everything to be ironed and our wooden floors to be polished. I remember we smaller kids would slide around on sheets pulled by the older siblings to help shine the floor in our socks.

Since we were a large family of eleven, we would take up the entire pew at church, and all eyes were on us. Our mother would sew her dresses, as well as all of us girls, with matching cotton fabric, and the boys had ironed white shirts that were crisp and spotless. For this reason, we were often late. One would never think we were hiding a family secret. Today, society would call our family dysfunctional because both of my parents were alcoholics. Functioning alcoholics. Monday through Friday my parents performed well in their jobs. The occasional weekend was a different story.

Our meticulously cleaned home with a manicured lawn and a fragrant lilac bush alongside the window, which was cracked open during summer months, was like a battleground on the weekends. Starting at 1:00 a.m. when the bars closed, and they would both come home intoxicated and fighting. We lived in a small two-bedroom house on Camas Street in a small town in Eastern Washington. A lot of us siblings slept all in a row on the floor, so I would get woken up with loud voices that would often startle me so strongly that fear would grip me.

I did not know that my body shaking and my heart racing—feeling like I could not breathe—were the first of many panic attacks I would come to know at such a young age. They would start up again when I was in my thirties. My young mind could not comprehend that there were happy times, such as Mom practicing a classical tune called "Für Elise" and one of my big sister's and I danced around her piano pretending to be ballerinas.

But then the weekend would come, and the fighting would ensue. I would cover my ears so tightly and hug my pillow in the grips of fear with my baby brother crying in the background. I begged them to please stop, but they could not hear me because they were so caught up in the heat of the moment that there was no coming back. One of my big brothers would take on the role of peace maker and come in between my quarreling parents, sending another sibling to call the police. There was a time when my parents' fighting was so violent that my dad was arrested and forced to leave our home. My mother's front teeth were knocked out at the hands of my father.

My older siblings protected me by keeping me from seeing my mom, who was sleeping for what I thought was such a long time. I missed my mom, so I snuck inside her room where she lay in deep slumber with the stench of alcohol breath. I saw her swollen, bloody face, and I was so scared because I did not know what had happened to her. As shocking as my family's story may seem, God in all His splendor would soon be orchestrating a big change for our family. I strongly believe someone prayed for our very troubled big family. The answers would soon follow in such a grand way.

When my father packed all his belongings in the back of the family car, he drove to the Seattle area to stay with family. My mother had what they called back then a nervous breakdown, and she was hospitalized. The doctor ordered complete bed rest for her. My older siblings took care of me. I remember the Catholic priest coming to check on all of us children and people bringing over food for us. After several months, my dad called my mom wanting to get back together. I think my mom was reluctant, but he said he found a good job and a big white house for us all to come live together as a family again. That's exactly what we did. We packed up everything in a truck my dad drove and the family station wagon.

FOUNDATIONAL TRUTHS

After we settled into our new home, we began attending Catholic Mass again. This was the beginning of God introducing Himself as Savior, Redeemer, and Prince of Peace.

> *"For God so loved the world that he gave his only begotten Son, so that whosoever believeth in him should not perish, but have everlasting life." (John 3:16, KJV)*

A foundational truth our family was in the process of being taught, even in the greatest turmoil, was that our God would show us how big He truly is. We surrendered and accepted our need for a Savior. Someone invited my mom to a prayer meeting in the gym of the Catholic church we were attending by a God-appointed, born-again Catholic priest. Weekly, my mom would come home crying. I thought something was wrong, so I asked her, and she explained they were happy tears. Every week I continued to see my mom come home after these prayer meetings incredibly happy and transforming right before my eyes into a new woman.

This was in the '70s when the Charismatic movement was at its peak. My mom got saved and filled with the Holy Spirit with the evidence of speaking in tongues. My dad soon followed. They both were instantly delivered from alcoholism and nicotine. My older brothers and sisters went with my parents and were also saved and filled with the Holy Spirit. The was the beginning of my family's transformation. The fire was ignited among the Catholic Church all over Seattle.

My parents were excited about a bigger prayer meeting taking place in the heart of Seattle, Washington. They even invited us children for a kid's service. Me and my younger brother Robert raised our hands when the teacher asked, "Who would like to ask Jesus to come into their heart?" We prayed the sinner's prayer. Afterward, my brother and I looked at each other with happy grins. I was only nine years old, and my little brother was five; nonetheless, it is a memory I shall never forget. From that launching point, I headed toward a personal relationship with my Savior God.

My young life was never the same again. The Bible says in Revelation 3:20 (NIV), *"Here I am! I stand at the door and knock.*

If anyone hears my voice and opens the door, I will come in and eat with that person, and they with me."

I vividly recall sitting in Mass in Catholic school when suddenly I heard someone calling my name, and it startled me. I turned around in all directions, but there was no one there. Right then in that moment, God was calling me by my name. I felt such peace. My Savior God would introduce Himself as my Prince of Peace.

I also remember in my third-grade class at that same school we had an assignment to write an essay on what *peace* means. In all my misspellings, I muttered out my experience of God calling me by name and the peace that followed. It was a contest, and during the Mass we had that week, the Catholic priest would call out the winner for each grade. One by one the winner was called up front on the platform. For my class, I did not win. This very smart, studious boy won, and he proudly marched forward when his name was called to get his certificate and his essay back.

When I sat in the church pew listening for when the priest called out my name, I didn't realize what was happening. My teacher motioned for me to go forward. I nervously approached the very seriously stoic priest sitting in his big ornate chair clad in his priestly attire. He began to speak to me. He said he really enjoyed my essay, and it was exceptionally good. He also said he wanted to choose my essay as the winner for my class, but there were many misspelled words and not written neatly. He then told me I could sit back down.

When I sat down, my teacher smiled at me. I was a very well-behaved shy girl. I felt like I did something good, and I was just speaking from my heart while I wrote. I believe when I first asked Jesus into my heart, I called His name, and He answered just as it says in His Word.

> *"Call to me and I will answer and tell you great unsearchable things you do not know." (Jeremiah 33:3, NIV)*

I believe the great and mighty things God was about to show me was that despite all that had occurred in my life—the dysfunction and domestic violence—He was God who was in control of all things. He would later show me I was chosen to be born into this family to make a difference.

The French Jesuit priests came to our continent to convert many Native American tribes to Christianity over three centuries ago. The Native Americans referred to the priests as, "The Black Robes." In fact, my younger brother Robert, who lived with my parents on our reservation at the time, had a summer job in his teen years helping to dig up the graves of these priests and move them from Saint Mary's Catholic Church to another location, placing them in pine boxes marked with identification. Many of the tribe's people were opposed to this. My brother said he could see their black priest robes with large rosaries with large ornate crosses and tassels, along with their black leather boots. Some of their skin was intact, mummified in appearance.

My great-grandfather, Andrew Seltice, was also a writer, and he wrote a book called *The Saga of the Coeur d'Alene Indians.*[1] To my surprise, I read that a prophet named Circling Raven prophesied that The Black Robes would come and bring a message of the coming Messiah. I leaped for joy inside because this meant he was for Christianity. My ancestors were for Jesus the coming Messiah. All the pieces were coming together before my eyes. I am to continue to preach the message that the Messiah, Jesus Christ, is coming back again in the Second Coming of the rapture of God's chosen people, natives and non-natives.

God was going to use me. One in my position might ask, "God, why didn't You rescue me from such calamity?" I do not remember asking Him; during the abusive years, I was just in survival mode and trying not tremble with crippling fear. That happened quite often at that time. In retrospect, I did wonder what my parents survived that would cause them to so passionately fight against each other.

I did know that my father came from a blended family. His mother, my grandmother, did have children from two marriages. The first to a man unknown to my dad because he was not his father. My grandmother then married my grandpa, Modesto, who crossed the border into the United States after he witnessed his father's execution in his homeland of Jalisco, Mexico. I was told the men saw my grandfather looking down into the courtyard where the murder took place.

That is why he fled at such a young age and joined the troops of the late Poncho Villa as his bugle boy but not before those men chased him from rooftop to rooftop, shooting at him. One bullet grazed his head and then landed in his foot where fragments stayed imbedded for many years. Toward the end of his life, he did end up losing both legs by amputation to the effects of diabetes and the pieces of metal left his foot.

My grandmother, Guadalupe Miramontez, had several children from her first marriage. She then had a common law second marriage to my grandfather, Modesto Miramontez. She gave birth to more children, which my dad was a product of. Often, he would feel the hurt of the past that was not dealt with and was suppressed. Because he did not receive the love he should have, it explained his inability to give outward affections of love to my mom or us kids.

My mom, on the other hand, had tragedies of her own, one of which was her feelings of being rejected by her mother. The other was her mother dying in an alcohol-related accident. When we went to Grandma Calla's (Clara Sherwood) house to make sense of what happened, we could see burn marks on the kitchen floor where her body had lain after catching fire by the stove with a bottle of vodka nearby. She had burned to death. Foul play was suspected since she just cashed her crop shares check from the land she owned. My mom did request for the investigation to be reopened, but we never heard anything back. The case was closed, and the funeral had to be closed casket.

As terribly graphic as this appears, it is necessary to know that we serve a God of restoration. It does not matter how deep the pain or how insensible it is. Even in these extreme life situations, nothing is too enormous for God to heal and a testimony to be told. My mom suffered years at the painful memory of her mother's passing, but glory to God she is in heaven in her new body with a new name and a crown of jewels. There is no sorrow in heaven. Knowing this reality is comforting. God's promises are yea and amen. He promises to give us beauty for ashes and a garment of praise for the spirit of heaviness. One of His promises I like the most is that what the enemy took from you He will return to you sevenfold. There is recompense, and payday is coming.

We may have lost my grandmother in a senseless death, but my parents were both blessed with so many grandchildren and great-grandchildren that my sister struggled to count them all in the eulogy given at their funerals. My father, John Madrenas Miramontez, passed away in March 2010, and my mom, Adrianna Miramontez, passed away in March 2014, both from diabetes complications. They are buried side by side at the tribal cemetery in Desmet, Idaho, with a grave marker with hearts joining them together. In running the race of life, we do come across grief and loss. Only with my faith in God All Mighty have I survived and have gotten back on track.

KNOWING WHO YOU ARE IN CHRIST

Even though my mom became a Christian, I did not see her living her life in complete victory. I believe she did suffer from a deep-rooted sense of inferiority. She had seen how people looked down on her for being a woman of color, and I could see that in her countenance. I learned from seeing her lack of self-worth, and when I see my own self-image, I look at what

God would desire for me to study in the scriptures about who I am in Christ Jesus.

- I am seated in heavenly places. Ephesians 2:6
- I am the apple of God's eye. Psalm 17:8
- I am chosen by God's doing. 1 Peter 2:9
- I am above and not beneath. I am the head and not the tail. Deuteronomy 28:13

Recently, I have gotten past depression and have started my artwork again. So, knowing that I'm God's masterpiece is personally rewarding (Ephesians 2:10). I now know how valuable I am to God. My oldest daughter wrote a poem in high school sharing who she believes she is.

I'M THE SPIRIT
BY MELISSA CURRY

I'm the spirit who roams our land
That now belongs to another man
I'm the spirit who cries at night,
Cries that one day we'll win the fight;
I'm the spirit who soars above,
With the eagles and native love;
I'm the spirit who roars frightened in the dark,
And finds comfort in the tree's rough bark;
I'm the spirit whose still in prayer,
And sends a breeze through your standing hair;
I'm the spirit, who makes you feel secure,
And loneliness' only cure;

I'm the spirit of all nations,
that lives for all precious creations;
I'm the spirit.

HAVE A GOOD SUPPORT SYSTEM

Just as a house is built with a durable support beam, having well-seasoned believers around is crucial to having success in our lives as well. Know who is in your cheering section. These are good, trusting friends who should be a small circle you keep nearby. They should never be afraid to speak the truth to you in love. They are people you can call upon for prayer and support. The Bible says, *"…not forsaking the assembling of ourselves together." (Hebrews 10:25, KJV)*

Furthermore, you should be just as mindful of who is *not* cheering for you from the sidelines. Any words anyone may say to you or about you that is not edifying or not spoken in love you should turn a deaf ear to. If you listen to negativity, you can question yourself or feel defeated. Your self-worth would be in danger of plummeting, which is the enemy's purpose to defeat you and pull you down so you will fall out of the race in life.

I have been amongst Christians in church giving a testimony of God's goodness about something great He had done for me that week. Many were encouraging and responded with an amen and a nod. However, on occasion, not everyone was happy for me when I experienced God's blessing. It is rather a shedding of light on their personal walk with God and a painful reminder of the lack of obedience in their own lives, which results in them not getting the blessing. So when someone else is receiving, it is difficult to applaud them.

How people react to your testimony does not change what you are giving voice to. I give testimony as part of the battle in spiritual warfare I shall overcome. I love bragging about God. It is all for His glory. He knows and understands me, and that is all that matters. If people are pouring out toxicity toward you, and that includes family members, cut them out of your race. Consider this: if you don't, it will slow you down.

> *"The Lord is righteous; he has cut me free from the cords of the wicked." (Psalm 129:4, KJV)*

SELF-REFLECTION

- While running the race, do you know that you have everything you need for success?
- Are you ready at the starting line?
- Have you considered the foundational truths?
- Do you know who you are in Christ Jesus?
- Finally, do you have a good support system?

CHAPTER TWO

FINDING YOUR FOOTING

GET CLEAR DIRECTION

Along your journey, you must be certain of finding your footing, be clear of the direction in which you are headed and know where you're coming from. While I was in college doing my prerequisites for the LPN to RN program, I wrote this poem in my English class:

WHERE I AM FROM

I am from integrity of the valley of a smooth proud mountain range, from long stretches of dirt roads, from rows upon rows of aromatic apple-filled orchards. I am from the strongest of organized linear hops and from sweat of hard labor from sunrise to sunset. I am from the sweetest of fresh-picked corn to the juiciest of red fat tomatoes. I am from the richness of quinceañeras and from the warmness of homemade tortillas.

I come from "cleanliness is next to godliness," from fresh-ironed clothes and polished shoes lined up from biggest to smallest placed near the furnace to dry, prepared for Sunday. I am from the spirit dancing through me in native song to the beat of my hand drum. I am from, "honk if you love Jesus!" to soft-spoken words in reverent prayer.

I am from easy laughter in the shelter of humor from something gone awry and from the joy on a sunny day. I am from running track meets in my first pair of Nikes, from volleyball games and spelling bees. I am from good grades and art projects, from student body secretary to teenage pregnancy. I am from high expectations to a statistic.

I am from Hall and Oats and leg warmers to Paula Abdul and hoop earrings. I am from finding the remote with my favorite cuddly throw, popcorn,

> *and diet Squirt, watching* The Waltons *and* Little House on the Prairie.
>
> *I am from the resilience of the brightest flowers once trampled to, "Look I am still standing." I am from the biggest of families, number seven little sister, and from the security of Daddy picking me up. I am from rolling down grassy hillsides with my little brother, from climbing cherry trees with my red-haired best friend. Her name was Kris, and she had freckles. I am from "Hey, Cousin, long time no see."*
>
> *I am from dishes and diapers, from mounds of laundry and meals to cook. I am from traveling miles across the states, staying in Motel 6, and living in Germany for three years as a dutiful military wife.*
>
> *I am from the sorrow of tragedy, and I am from the little girl who loved Raggedy Ann and Andy. I am from a battlefield against oppression, from warriors and soldiers that did not win. I am from borders my grandfather crossed, from determination in my grandmother's photo. Most of all, I am from Creator God.*

When continuing on life's path, you can acknowledge your past and forgive those you need to, but you must go forward and not look back lest you turn into a pillar of salt.

"But his wife looked back from behind him, and she became a pillar of salt." (Genesis 19:26, KJV)

You must focus on where you are headed and beware of any danger lurking. Notice that deer in the wild may stop to eat, but they are always on hinds' feet ready to flee in a moment's notice when danger is evident. Their heads turn in different directions to be aware for their safety.

On life's journey, we need to have the same alertness to anything that appears suspicious. We also must position ourselves for success and be alert just the same. Knowing where you are going is also very key. You must have a plan. When I was doing college courses, I enjoyed my English class immensely. This is the other half of my poem.

WHERE I AM GOING

I am going to walk down sterile hallways in stride with dutiful purpose, smelling medicine and body fluids, wearing scrubs and tucking my hair into a cap. I am going to patient charts, stethoscopes, and elastic gloves. I am going to hold the hand of one with a grimace of pain and to comfort suffering families of lost loved ones. I am going to tell them of the One who heals.

I am going to write a book, telling of my life's story of grief and loss to triumph and victory. I am going to give encouragement and pick one up. I am going to have healthy living and run a marathon. I am going to the creative curve of my signature, and I am going to paint oil on canvas. I am going to that place where my works are created, displaying shelf upon shelf of the best clay shaping that many will like.

I am going to the Holy Land, Disneyland, Florida, and Hawaii too. I am going to own my first House. My daughter saw it in a dream once. I said, "Oh yes, that will be mine one day; it will be true." I am going to have a brand-new car driven only by me. I going to have the security of a retirement and savings plan, and I will have no worries, don't you see? I am going to all that my Father has promised me. "The best is yet to come."

I am going to turn fifty this year it is true, but my life is not half over because I am going to new beginnings and increase. Stay and be my friend, and you will see it happening with all the expectation of this life ahead. I am going to conquer mountains and many Goliaths because I am strong, you see. I am going to continue walking in steps ordered from above with head lifted high in confidence because I am going to be as bold as a lion, my Father said so, and He does not lie. I am going to shine like the brightest of diamonds in the sky. Stick around and you will see that I am honesty and do not lie.

PERSPECTIVE

What are you looking at? How do you think? Do you dwell on what others think of you or what they have said about you? Does what you think about line up with the Word of God? The Bible says, "For as he thinketh in his heart, so is he" (Proverbs 23:7, KJV). In my effort to have the right perspective, I have studied the scriptures immensely. I would pray to God for help with this area as well. However, throughout my day it seems like the enemy of my soul would attempt to detour me in my thinking.

Thoughts of offense and deep wounds of the past would come up for no reason. I did not ask for it. I found myself rebuking the devil. I would speak the Word back to him, and he would flee just as the Word says. I was even more determined to gain victory over this, so I would listen to sermons on TV.

I finally decided to begin considering what Joyce Meyer had to say because she came from a background of sexual abuse as I did, so I listened to her and bought many of her books and CDs. The one that ministered to me was *The Battlefield of the Mind.* Through reading her book, I learned a great deal.

DISCERNMENT

In one of my art classes in college, one of my assignments was a self-portrait. I painted myself with a tee pee where my nose is with smoke going through the top of my head. Then across the front of my T-shirt was a background with arrows shooting across from an Indian on a horse. On each arrow were the names of the oppressions we battle against: alcoholism, depression, drug addiction, suicide, shorter life expectancy, high infant mortality, teen pregnancy, illiteracy, unemployment.

I did not know it then, but this was prophetic because I stood up in church thinking I was giving a testimony, referring to my painting, but then, with the Holy Spirit prompting me, I began speaking a word that these were all the strongholds that were being torn down as I spoke. God is our mighty warrior. We surrender to Him, and He fights our battles. The battle is not ours to fight. Hallelujah!

However, knowing that the battle belonged to the Lord did not come easily. Because of the sin in my life and not walking a perfect walk, I did not think I was worthy. The enemy was telling me lies, and I believed it and listened to them. I really had to study the scripture in the Joyce Meyer teachings and believe it in order to have victory over my mind.

I believe that having witnessed domestic violence growing up I began experiencing panic attacks after my first husband left our seventeen-year marriage with four children. My firstborn teenage daughter attempted suicide because she could not deal with the pain. The ambulance was taking her to the emergency room at the nearest hospital, and I was having chest pain for the first time in my adult life. My doctor diagnosed me with posttraumatic stress disorder, depression, and adult attention deficit disorder (ADD). This was the first time I had to begin taking medication daily, and it was a turning point in my life.

MORAL COMPASS

In the aftermath of the divorce in my first marriage, I did not turn to God at first. I did not think I was worthy. My self-esteem was at an all-time low. I could not even get out of bed for two weeks, nor could I keep anything in my stomach. If I ate anything, I would soon vomit. My children's father was my high school sweetheart. He was my first love and the one I lost my virginity to, so the end of this marriage made me feel like I could not exist without him. I did not want the divorce. He had been using drugs, and he was not coming home after work. He began working at a bar, which was a big mistake for our marriage.

I made an ultimatum. I said, "Either you stop what you are doing or leave." I thought he would most definitely choose me and the kids, but he did not. He left, and I was still recovering from injuries I had suffered from a car accident we had been involved in. It was also two weeks before Christmas, so the timing could not have been worse, but I survived. Even though I did not reach out to God for help, He was waiting for me. I just did not know it.

At that time, I judged my ex-husband on his choice to leave me for another woman and the drug lifestyle, and I was heartbroken. I did turn my back on the Lord God momentarily. I did frequent the bar scene on the weekends as an escape, as well as some failed relationships. It is not something I am proud of, but ultimately, I did come to my senses. I realized that my parents were alcoholics in my young childhood years, and my grandmother did die in a tragic alcohol-related accident. I was now a single mother of four children, and waking up with hangovers and trying to recover the next day was just not worth it. The responsibility on my shoulders was sobering enough.

Even though someone else was not doing what was right, and the terrible choice they made was life-altering to the family, does not mean that you cannot be the bigger person and do what is morally correct. And that is what I had decided to do. I reset my moral compass, so to speak, but more importantly, I wanted to be led by the Spirit of God. When running this race of life, you may get off track. As Maya Angelou once said, "Do the best you can until you know better. Then when you know better, do better."[2] You may need to take out your compass and say to yourself, "It is now time to get back on track," as well as pray and surrender to God, knowing that you cannot do this single parenting alone. You most definitely need His redirecting.

BETRAYAL

Sometimes in life one of the challenges you may face is being betrayed by someone you once loved. In facing a situation that you never thought would ever happen, it can leave you in total shock. I have heard it once said that divorce is like a death, and I would agree. After deciding that the drinking and party scene was not the answer to my new set of problems, I decided that it was time to seek a good church. I believe that this was a God-orchestrated moment indeed.

The church that I found had a single mom's group. I knew this would be good for me, and they were very loving and accepting. This was just what I needed. However, I also was now feeling very bitter and resentful because this was a group that I did not ever think I would belong to. The social stigma of single parenting left me feeling terribly angry. I was prideful, and it was hard for me to admit that I was now alone and needed help. My integrity was now at stake, and all I could do was just try to be strong for my children and do the best I could. Attending this church helped me to get back to the basics of biblical truths.

GOOD GROUND

When running the race of life, having good ground is the most important for success in what you sow. Let us look at the parable of the sower, where we can learn about the three types of soil.

> *"Then he told them many things in parables, saying: farmer went out to sow his seed. As he was scattering the seed, some fell along the path, and the birds came and ate it up. Some fell on rocky places, where it did not have much soil. It sprang up quickly, because the soil was shallow. But when the sun came up, the plants were scorched, and they withered because they had no root. Other seed fell among thorns, which grew up and choked the plants. Still other seed fell on good soil, where it produced a crop—a hundred, sixty or thirty times what was sown." (Matthew 13:3–8, NIV)*

In my life's journey, I often ask my Father God for wisdom and knowledge to use the seed, which is the Word of God, to plant and cultivate it according to His perfect will. In all my actions, what is my intent when witnessing to others and sowing the seed given to me? Am I doing it for my own benefit because I want them to believe the way I believe? If I am not considering what I am saying and just doing without much thought or no time praying or time in Bible study, then the seed plant could be on rocky places or thorny ground, neither of which are any benefit to anyone. Then it dies.

On the other hand, sowing seed where it is a God-ordained moment and the door is open for you to be a witness, then this is good ground, and the result is a great outcome, such as salvation to one's soul and a life is saved. This outcome is fruitful indeed, and God is glorified. Take note of where you see that the soil is rich. I was born in Eastern Washington, which is known to be a farming community. This was where my parents met, both taking advantage at that time of the ample employment opportunity in that region. Many know that the Toppenish–Yakima area is where you can find the best produce because of the richness in soil.

CONFIDENCE

Being certain of oneself is an attribute necessary for success on the journey of life. It is one of the many characteristics of the virtuous woman spoken of in Proverbs 31. When I first read about this woman of God, my first thought was that I could never measure up. However, as I have matured and have gone from glory to glory, God changed and transformed me into a new woman. A lot of healing has taken place, and my personal relationship with Him has never been closer. When I peer into the mirror at myself getting ready for work or church, I see a middle-aged woman, but now also one with the many virtues as this woman.

> *Verse 10: "Who can find a virtuous woman? For her price is far above rubies."*
>
> *Verse 12: "She will do him good and not evil all the days of her life."*
>
> *Verse 15: "She riseth also while it is yet night, and giveth meat to her household, and a portion to her maidens."*
>
> *Verse 22: "She maketh herself coverings of tapestry; her clothing is silk and purple."*
>
> *Verse 23: "Her husband is known in the gates, when he sitteth among the elders of the land."*
>
> *Verse 25: "Strength and honour are her clothing; and she shall rejoice in time to come."*
>
> *Verse 27: "She looketh well to the ways of her household, and eateth not the bread of the idleness."*
>
> *Verse 28: "Her children arise up, and call her blessed; her husband also, and he praiseth her."*
>
> *(Proverbs 31:10–31, KJV)*

When you read this passage, did you see all her attributes? She looks like a woman who was always providing well for her husband and her children, always working with her hands, and everything was taken care of. She was artistic and well-dressed in silk and purple. She never slept in, waking up in the dawn hours before the sun rose. Notice how everything she put her hand to was blessed. She was appreciated as her children called her blessed, and her husband praised her. She was known in her community. No doubt this woman did well in her race of life.

SELF-REFLECTION

- Do you have a clear direction in your race of life? If not, think about it and write in your journal. What is it you are lacking?
- Do you know where you are going?
- Consider seeds you have sown. Which of the three types of soil is the ground where you've sown?
- What attributes of the virtuous woman do you possess currently? Which ones are you asking God to continue to develop in you?

CHAPTER THREE

TAKE OFF

In running your life's journey, you have done many things to prepare for this portion, and that's good, but now it's the time to go. It may seem scary, but for myself, I remembered my mother's words, and I took off and ran like a deer, or what I imagined a deer like. Just do everything you know how to. There is no time to procrastinate or think of any other way. Now is the time. We serve a "Now God." If you wait for another time, it may become a missed opportunity. All of your preparation has paid off, and now you are ready. Remember, you can do this, just as God's Word says: *"I can do all things through Christ who strengthens me." (Philippians 4:13, NKJV)*

In one of my favorite movies, *Forrest Gump*, Jenny says, "Run, Forrest!" Do you recall what happened when he began running? His leg braces fell off, and he began running even faster. He forgot that he supposedly had limitations; however, as he acted, I believe the good Lord blessed his efforts and healed him completely. That was the last of those leg braces that formerly bound him. When we are proactive, God blesses what we put our hand to. *"He makes my feet like the feet of deer, and sets me on high places." (2 Samuel 22:34, NKJV)*

ENDURANCE

It is most important that we have the strength to be able to finish the race set before us as well as the stamina to be able to keep going no matter how difficult or how tired may become.

Oxford Dictionary's definitions are:

> (n) the fact or power of enduring an unpleasant or difficult process or situation without giving way.
>
> (adj) denoting or relating to a race or other sporting event that takes place over a long distance or otherwise demands great physical stamina. "the annual 24 endurance race."[3]

The temptation may come to just give up, but there's great reward if we finish. We never want to be defeated because we just could not handle the unpleasantness. It is a long process, no doubt. Hardship is not easy, but it is something we can choose to endure. If we endure, then we can finish. Let us take a look at another scripture.

"I have fought the good fight, I have finished the course, I have kept the faith." (2 Timothy 4:7, KJV)

This scripture reminds us of what takes place when we finish when it says "I have kept the faith." Faith is the result of the strength we get from finishing. How we finish is by enduring. Having this type of discipline comes a little easier for me because I had a father who was hardworking, and I would see him endure hardships repeatedly from sunrise to sunset. When I was incredibly young and we lived in a farming community in Eastern Washington, my father would bring me and my little brother to my grandpa Modesto's for him to babysit us. He did not speak any English, but my little brother and I caught on to what he was saying in Spanish.

It seemed like such a long day before my dad would come get us. Grandpa would listen to the Spanish station after we had a dinner of beans, rice, and homemade tortillas. I would stare out the window until I could see from a distance the headlights of my dad's car coming from a long stretch of dirt road. When came into the house I could tell he was tired. His coveralls were dirty and so was his sweaty face. I was so happy to see him that I would grab his legs and hug him.

He would sit and eat some dinner and talk to Grandpa in Spanish, which was becoming more familiar to me and my little brother. Later in my adult life when hard times came, I knew what to do. I did not complain. I knew I had to take care of my children alone after my husband, the father of our children, abandoned us. God's Word says, *"The one who is unwilling to work shall not eat." (2 Thessalonians 3:10, NIV)*

My dad had eleven mouths to feed, so he most definitely worked hard for all of us to eat without complaining. If he was tired, he did not say so. When I had four children from my first marriage to take care of and feed alone as a single parent, working was awfully hard to do in those circumstances, but I pushed forward and did it.

PERSEVERANCE

Being persistent is what kept me going. It was good work ethics repeated, even in difficult times. Delays may come and setbacks are inevitable, but you just refocus and, with fortitude, keep going. Delays happen at times, but you just get back on track the best you can. From experience, achievements and success are always in your future when you don't quit. God blesses your efforts, but you must stay in your race.

When we stand before God on the Day of Judgment, you will be asked what you did with your assignment. How did you run your race? How did you use your gifts and talents? I want to be able to stand before my Father God and give an account of the race I ran, the race that was only for me. My anointing is just for me. It is nontransferable.

I want to be able to celebrate all my accomplishments with Him for His glory and the edification of His body. All came into being from not giving up and persevering. I had the tenacity of not letting go of the momentum I worked so hard to keep going in the face of adversity. It was all for the kingdom of God because I am of a royal priesthood. Being a daughter of King Jesus has had great benefits because He breathed life over my endeavors in this race of life and made it the success that it is today. Glory to God!

AUTOPILOT

There are times when difficult situations come at you that you did not plan on. The going gets very exhausting and begins to slow you down. The setback may get in the way of progress. In those times, you may be tempted to just put yourself in autopilot mode, where you may think that nothing good will happen and you are not expecting anything but more bad news to come. So as tired as you are you just keep going in an almost a zombie-like state. Beware! This sort of thinking is unhealthy and does not line up with the Word of God.

> *If we confess our sins, He is faithful and just to forgive us our sins and to cleanse us of all unrighteousness. (1 John 1:9, NKJV)*

In the past, I thought I was not worthy to pray and ask God for help. I had failed Him once again. The Bible says, *"The steadfast love of the Lord never ceases; his mercies never come to an end; they are new every morning." (Lamentations 3:22–23, ESV)* There is no limit to how many times we are forgiven.

I believe you have to say no to wrong thinking patterns and remember who our friend is. *"... And there is a friend that sticketh closer than a brother." (Proverbs 18:24, KJV)* He is the reason there is mercy available to us. We must recognize our need for a Savior. *"For he hath made him to be sin for us, who knew no sin; that we might be made the righteousness of God in him." (2 Corinthians 5:21, KJV)*

He became the sacrificial Lamb without spot or wrinkle, so that we could be saved. (1 Peter 1:9) If we do not stop and consider all of God's promises, we can become weary, and we may even be tempted to listen to the enemy, who is the accuser of the brethren. We should always strengthen ourselves throughout our journeys with prayer and the Word of God.

"Give ear to my words, O Lord, consider my meditation. Hearken unto the voice of my cry, my King, and my God: for unto thee will I pray. My voice shalt thou hear in the morning, O Lord; in the morning will I direct my prayer unto thee, and will look up." (Psalm 5:1–3, KJV) It is God's voice we want to hear, so we must always be tuned in so we can hear what the Spirit is saying and not the deceiver.

Finally, another danger in not being in tune with the Spirit of God is pride. *"Pride goes before destruction, and a haughty spirit before a fall." (Proverbs 16:18, NIV)* When we are not in right standing with God, we may have the tenancy to think we have to do everything in our own strength. I believe there is a God-shaped hole in all of us. That is how much He wants us.

Only He can fill the void we once had in our lives before we were fully surrendered to Him as our Lord and Savior. Once we have a full understanding of our need for our Savior Jesus Christ and are fully committed to Him to lead our lives, then we can be completely devoted and satisfied in Him. This accomplishment is another mile ran and closer to the prize.

CHAPTER FOUR

BUCK UP

BETRAYAL

There was a time in my life when I was going through a rough time. I had just given up my job of twelve years because they said if I did not quit, they would fire me. I felt like I had no choice but to give my resignation from my family's only source of income as a housekeeper at a large reputable hospital. I had suffered a lot of missed work and was tardy due to the stress of being a single mom coupled with chronic migraine headaches and absences from my four children at home.

Had I only known that I was not alone, I could have just asked for help, as His Word says so. The sting of divorce had me convinced that I could not pray and receive and get answers. I'm so thankful that His Word tells us otherwise. *"Let us therefore come boldly unto the throne of grace, that we may obtain mercy, and find mercy, and find grace in a time of need." (Hebrews 4:16, KJV)*

The children were suffering and not turning to the One who heals. My first two daughters were teenagers, struggling with the divorce, attending school, and just wanting to be normal teenagers. This meant rebellion against me by them throwing parties in our house, which I would later hear about from my neighbors. My third eldest daughter, a preteen, slipped into a deep depression and sudden weight gain from all that was going around her. My toddler son adjusted to his dad not being there any longer. I was going to school full time to reach a goal I had set to become a registered nurse—my dream job.

No amount of medicine was adequate to get ahead of the constant pain of these headaches. This line of work was physically demanding on my body. Three out of the twelve years I worked there I was their check-out/project housekeeper on the graveyard shift, 10:30 p.m. to 6:30 a.m. I performed floor and carpet care as well as stopping to clean a discharged room if needed. I injured my back a few times. I was prideful and competitive because that was what I was taught to do by my dad. Remember, God's Word warns us of pride: "*Pride goes before destruction, a haughty spirit before a fall." (Proverbs 16:18, NIV)*

Even so, my boss did not understand or appreciate me. I always had this feeling that my work was never good enough and that he had such a distain for me, as did a handful of coworkers who did not sympathize with me; they talked about me. I had to quit school because my grades were suffering, and I was in a deep depression. My life was in chaos.

I had to begin working at a new job as a waitress at the local Indian casino. To my relief, the bad headaches stopped. I had thought I could do this job, even though it had been thirteen years since I did this kind of work. I did the best I could, but I was not incredibly good at it. Previously when I waitressed, I hand wrote all my food orders and put them through to the kitchen manually. Now with computers, we entered all the orders through the computer, which I was just learning myself.

However, in my waitress job at the casino, occasionally my order was not entered properly in their system. When I pressed the SEND button, something went wrong, and the order would disappear. This isn't good when people are waiting for their food. It was a catastrophe for me, and they were not very nice about the whole situation. I was hard on myself, and I felt very foolish and embarrassed.

After one of these ordeals, I was called into the office of the Food and Beverage Department. While they were talking to me, telling me this was not working out, I broke into tears. I was so upset with myself. I really wanted this job to work. One of the two managers working with me said, "If you are going to work in the restaurant industry, you are going to have to buck up." I remember thinking how offensive those words were to me. If she only knew where I was coming from and how important this job was for me.

They ended up moving me to the deli, where I was a cashier. This job worked out for a while until I found a better paying job. It certainly does take one with a backbone to be able to work in the food industry in a casino with the smoke-filled environment. This was not for me, and I most definitely learned that the grass was not greener on the other side. *"Be kind to one another, tenderhearted, forgiving one another, as God in Christ forgave you." (Ephesians 4:32, ESV)*

Naturally I am a tenderhearted person. Society says, "Do not wear your heart on your sleeve," but my Christian beliefs say be of a tender heart, which I am. However, the Bible also says to guard your heart. *"Keep thy heart with all diligence; for out of it are the issues of life." (Proverbs 4:23, KJV)*

I have learned that there lies a healthy balance. I am nobody's doormat, but I most definitely do not say anything that grieves the Holy Spirit. As I have become a well-seasoned Christian, I am sensitive to never saying anything that does not reflect the character of God. There is a built-in filter that stops me from saying anything that is not loving or that does not edify or uplift. The fruits of the spirit are alive and well in me. Glory to God. God is good. All the time.

GRIEF AND LOSS

There are times in the race in life when you will have to deal with the loss of your parents, a significant other, family members, or those you considered family.

> *"To everything there is a season, and a time to every purpose under heaven; A time to be born, and a time to die; a time to plant and a time to pluck up that which is planted; A time to kill, and a time to heal; a time to break down, and a time to build up; A time to weep, and a time to laugh; a time to mourn, and a time to dance." (Ecclesiastes 3:1–4, KJV)*

My best friend Lorna died a little before my parents' passing, and that was a shocking loss for me. At church, I normally I go to worship God and hear a good sermon, only this time, it was for a funeral that I was not expecting. Profoundly serious faces filled the entry way with lots of handmade memorial photos of her with flowers. Everyone wore red, black, and white memorial T-shirts with of picture of her in her younger years. The lingering familiar odor of formaldehyde—the embalming fluid I had come to know from working at the hospitals—was coming from my friend, who lay in her casket.

As I approached, her sister was bravely fixing her Pendleton blanket around her body, wincing back tears. I made myself go to her coffin, still in disbelief, and I peered down into her casket. It was a moment that I thought would be unbearable, but just at that moment, the Holy Spirit showed up and encompassed me with such love and peace, like fluffy soft cotton clouds all around me. Her body did not look like her at all. She was wearing her Native American regalia, and I thought that was appropriate for who she was. She was like me, part Mexican American and part Native American, and that was much of how we bonded.

Her dad went to the same high school as my dad. I was not happy with the makeup job the funeral home had done. It was too dark, the lipstick was not something she would have not worn, and I do not know why I was distracted with the details. She and I connected well in fashion, and she would often tell me to come visit her because she had some clothes to give me. One time, she had just made some pozole she wanted to share with me. She wanted to clear out her closet because she was getting ready to go shopping and wanted to have some girlfriend time.

When I did take delight in her generosity, she asked, "Do you like it, sister?"

I said, "Heck yeah!"

She would let out this deep little chuckle that I miss hearing to this day. I still have held on to some of those pieces of clothing from her. I was not consumed because my Father God said I would not be. I survived that loss. Praise God for His Word that never fails to uplift me.

> *"To appoint them that mourn in Zion, to give them unto them beauty for ashes, the oil of joy for mourning, the garment of praise for the spirit of heaviness; that they might be called trees of*

righteousness, the planting of the Lord, that he might be glorified." (Isaiah 61:3, KJV)

I love my mom and dad, of course, but I thought they would always be here. I did not know I could live my life without them. It has been exceedingly difficult. There have been times when something good would happen, and I almost picked up the phone to call them and share it with them like before. My dad passed first in March of 2010. This was all if a sudden from stage 4 renal failure. My mother passed away four years later from diabetes complications. I went through all the stages of grief. I cried when I needed to. I am thankful for God's promises. *"Weeping may endure for a night, but joy cometh in the morning." (Psalm 30:5, KJV)*

What was unexpected for me coming from a large family was the different ways all my siblings and I have grieved. Many of us stood strong and didn't cry openly, while some of us cried at the grave site and not at the funeral. One of my older brothers became very weak with trembling and wanted to wander off to sit under a tree, since the tribal cemetery is more private than others.

Still, my younger brother who helped make the arrangements told me that after arriving at the cemetery to pick out the grave plot, he had his private time to have a good cry by himself. Then there was my youngest brother who took it the worst; while two hours had passed and we were all leaving, he wanted to linger and stay there with them. It was an incredibly sad scene seeing him from a distance standing there alone on their grave site, crying bitterly alone. We do not ever have to do this alone. In our weakness, He is strong.

> *"And he said unto me, my grace is sufficient for thee: for my strength is made perfect in weakness. Most gladly therefore will I rather glory in my infirmities, that the power of Christ may rest upon me." (2 Corinthians 12:9, KJV)*

When the holidays came, that was the saddest time for me. Even today, I find the holidays sad, and it has been a while since their passing. On Father's Day, I always miss my dad, and I usually post a picture of him on Facebook and honor him, as well as my mother on Mother's Day. we had a good father–daughter relationship. He was not as openly affectionate as I would have liked him to be, and there were times when he disciplined me with a belt because that was how he was raised. He was the best father he knew how to be. After he changed his life and became a believer, he did have regrets. The pastor of the church he had attended at that time told him that he needed to sit us adult children down and tell us that he was sorry.

I am okay about this not taking place because I have forgiven him as well as others in my family who needed forgiveness. The truth is that I have learned my language of love. I know through reading *The Five Love Languages* by Gary Chapman that my love language is acts of service. If someone does an act of kindness by helping me out with something that is difficult for me to do alone, then I really feel loved because they have just made my life easier by helping me. I had seen my dad come home from work very tired, and I knew that he loved me because he provided food and shelter for all nine of his children.

My older sister, on the other hand, has a different love language. Hers is acts of affection. She needs to be told that she is loved, or she would benefit from someone leaving her a love note. My dad would never have done that because he grew up not having been loved openly and affectionately, so he did not learn such normal displays of affection and was not comfortable giving it. The negative outcome, unfortunately, was that my older sister never felt that my dad really loved her. My mom never required loving affection of him from what I remember because that was also not something given to her openly as well. She was raised in a Catholic nun's convent.

I had to also deal with the loss of my dog, Vixie, not long after my mother's passing, and I must say that that was just as difficult as losing my mother. I has such deep sorrow and a lot of guilt because I blamed myself for her getting struck by a car. I could pay for her surgery to repair the injuries, and her quality of life thereafter would not be something to keep her alive—she had a broken pelvis. I was so heartbroken about my dog's passing that I could not get another dog until about five years later.

It had finally been arranged to have my parents in the same nursing home facility for about a month. My older sister had called me and told me that my dad had passed away after taking an afternoon nap with my mom in the nursing home in Yakima, Washington. They took my mom out of the room, and then they worked on him, performing three rounds of resuscitation to no avail. They called his death.

I remember calling my church for prayer about Dad's passing. I started to cry hysterically, but then I distinctly heard the voice of God tell me, "He's with Me now." I instantly felt peace, and when I looked around my room, it looked very luminous and glowing with a gentle rocking of the Holy Spirit all encompassing. I shall never forget that precious moment. Then I remembered my prayer request and most definitely felt their prayers.

The next day, I was still feeling a sense of peace and no sadness. I was sitting in my living room watching TV and just relaxing when from my peripheral vision I saw a being, who l looked like they were wearing a sort of costume because there something extending from both sides. I quickly looked and it disappeared, so I resumed watching TV. Then this being came back around the corner as if to check on me. It felt like such a sweet presence just watching over me. This time, I turned my head to look even faster, only this time I did see it was a white figure with the wing tip still visible as it ran down the hallway. I was so awestruck that God would send an angel, or angels, to camp around my apartment to minister to me at my father's passing. That is another amazing event that I shall never forget. My faith was strengthened.

I did feel that God was near but also that I needed time to heal. I wanted to stay near home until the time was right to be social again and be around people. I made sure that the time did not linger on past unhealthy grieving. I also spent time in prayer and in His Word, so that the enemy would not have a foothold in which to enter and cause havoc in my family. It was suggested to me to seek counsel, and I opted not to. I did not see anything out of the normal period of grieving, and there were no issues to deal with, so I sought comfort in a close group of church friends, who were willing to listen to me if I needed to speak. They would ask how I was doing, and I would honestly answer that I was adjusting without my dad as best as I knew how, and that I knew God was in control.

DISTRACTIONS

There will be times when you are running your race when there will be side fires from the left and from the right that you did not even see coming. At first, your direction seemed so clear and straight ahead, but then there comes this detour that you did not plan on. You must be alert and vigilant to know where the root of those distractions is coming from and the intent behind them. *"You were running well. Who hindered you from obeying the truth?" (Galatians 5:7, ESV)*

The distractions assigned against you and your family were meant to throw you off your God-ordained destiny. Immediately you must reposition yourself and get right back to your journey as strong as before with even more zeal and determination; you must finish your race.

Sometimes you might look at how others are running their race, but there's caution in that as well. Remember what happened in the story of David and Goliath when David tried to wear someone else's armor. It was too big and uncomfortable. He could not wear it. Never compare yourself to someone else's race, or wish you had what they have. You will never be happy if you are looking at what someone else has. We have been given the keys to the kingdom, so we have what it takes.

> *"And I will give unto thee the keys of the kingdom of heaven: and whatsoever thou shalt bind on earth shall be bound in heaven: and whatsoever thou shalt loose on earth shall be loosed in heaven." (Matthew 16:19, KJV)*

We all miss the mark daily, hence our need for our Savior dying on the cross. His last words as He died were, *"It is finished." (John 19:30, KJV)* It is a done deal. When you sin, just repent of it. Bring it before Father God.

> *"The Lord is compassionate and gracious, slow to anger, abounding in love...He does not treat us as our sins deserve or repay us according to our iniquities...As far as the east is from the west, so far has he removed our transgressions from us." (Psalm 103:8, 10, 12, NIV)*

I have one family member who will not receive Christ's forgiveness for their sins. This resistance is the same as saying what Jesus did for me, dying on the cross, was not enough, so I must do something myself and carry this anger and self-hatred to my deathbed and punish myself because that is what I deserve. I would love to see my beloved set free and living in victory, but right now it is not the case. There is not a thing I can do with this loved one's stubbornness, so I have brought this person to throne of grace and left my loved one there at the feet of Jesus. I do have hope. However, God's Word warns us about self-righteousness.

> *"But we are all as an unclean thing and all our righteousness's are as filthy rags; and we all do fade as a leaf; and our iniquities, like the wind, have taken us away." (Isaiah 64:6, KJV)*

LOSING SIGHT OF YOUR DREAM

Ever since I was a little girl, I knew I wanted to be a nurse and help people. I have seen my mother working in the medical field as a medical assistant. I had it all planned out after going through my first divorce that I needed to make better money. However, the combination of working full time, going to school full time, and meeting the needs of the family as a single parent became too much, and I needed to put my educational pursuits on hold. I was ridiculously hard on myself and lost all hope. I suffered in a deep depression for years. I was a Christian and saved but not walking in victory.

> *"Hope deferred maketh the heart sick: but when the desire cometh, it is a tree of life." (Proverbs 13:12, KJV)*

When I stopped going to school, I lost sight of a dream I once had. I learned that when plan A does not work, sometimes with God's plan B is better. I wanted to see again, because at that time, I had felt like I was like a rodent going around and around going nowhere but getting very tired quickly. I prayed for God to show me a sign or a vision, because I had read in His Word about the importance of a vision.

> *"Where there is no vision, the people perish: but he that keepeth the law, happy is he." (Proverbs 29:18, KJV)*

And the Bible says to write down your dream as well. Hallelujah!

> *"Then the Lord answered me and said, 'Write the vision and engrave it plainly on [clay] tablets so that the one who reads will run.'" (Habakkuk 2:2, AMP)*

SELF-REFLECTION

- Is there grief and loss that you are going through?
- Are there personal distractions that have thrown you off your course that you need to be aware of?
- Have you lost sight of your dream?

CHAPTER FIVE

GETTING KNOCKED DOWN

There have been times in my life early on when something situations were so traumatic that I needed an intervention by means of family counseling. I do not know if family counseling was within reach to my parents, who did their best to raise nine children. Those perilous times served a purpose, and it was not my time to leave this earth and die, so that is how I know that God saved my life many times. It was because of His divine plan and purpose for my life that I needed to be here for the fulfillment.

He chose the imperfect family I would be born into. He chose the parents I would have. I was the one to make a difference in my family, and I can see that now. I feel dutifully honored to be a part of an intervention of the God kind because all of the dysfunctions had to stop here at my generation and not be carried on in our bloodline to my children or grandchildren.

The first incident was a near drowning on a family outing along the Oregon coast at Rooster Rock State Park. I was only four years old, and my family and I were enjoying a beautiful sunny day with a scrumptious picnic and swimming. One of my older siblings summoned for my other sister and me to come and eat. My big sister and I went back into the water to wash off the sand, and then a strong undercurrent swept me off my feet and carried me off into the deep water that flowed over my head.

I did not know how to swim yet, so I kept swallowing lots of water. I remember going down, and then my body would temporarily surface above water. All I could see was my sister running up and down the beach screaming for someone to help. I started to sink deeper, and the water grew colder and darker to where I could not see, and I was so scared. Then suddenly out of nowhere, a strong man swam up under me, grabbed my legs, and brought me out of the water with ease. What a relief to my sister, who was so frightened and panicked. I did not drown that day because my Father God had a destiny for my life. That man who saved me was most certainly a godsend.

Even during such an event taking place, God's plans never changed. He would make my life be such that His Word prevailed in me, and His light did shine all around the people I was to influence for His glory. He helped me live it in my life.

There was another event that took place when I was about five years of age. I was playing at my friend Jill's house, and she wanted to go to the store to buy some candy. I thought that would be a fun thing to do. There was a busy street to cross, and she made it across the street safely. I could not see past the parked cars where I was standing, so she looked both ways for me and told me that it was clear for me to cross.

I trusted her word and ran quickly across the street. But there was a car coming, and it struck me. I was so little he did not even see me because it was the side of his car that hit me. He left the scene of the accident. I remember getting the wind knocked out of me, so for a moment I could not breathe. I was crying and lying there on the pavement. I looked up and saw a glimpse of my friend very scared, and she ran off back home.

I also saw an old lady with white hair, a flowered cotton dress with a matching sweater, and she was standing there with her arms outstretched for me to come to her. I was able to breathe, get up, and run to her. When I hugged her, I got blood all over her summery dress, but she didn't mind. She just wanted to give me some loving affection, which I greatly needed because of how scared I was. I just cried and cried in her arms. To this day, I think that maybe that was an angel of God sent to minister to me in that moment.

My lips were bleeding, and I skinned up my hands and knees. Some people at the church—right on that corner—also saw what had happened and wanted to help me, so they took me inside of their church and cleaned me up. One of them said, "I think I know where she lives," and they walked me home. I was going into shock, and I was physically shaking. I blankly stared ahead with no emotion.

I remember I was just not able to respond as people asked me questions. I was sitting on the coach, and I remember my mom was so mad at me for crossing the busy street, so she scolded me. I did what she said to do and just sat there with this blood-stained shirt, and my older sister was just looking at me. She asked my mom, "What's wrong with her?"

My mom said, "She's fine. Just wait until Dad gets home."

I remember just trembling, and I could not stop. I stared blankly ahead in shock. I thought I really did something wrong, and it was all my fault because my mom would not come near me to comfort me. I thought of myself as a bad girl.

Finally, my dad came home from work. He came and picked me up, and I held on to him, instantly feeling better with Dad home. Someone called the police, so I remember the policeman coming into our living room. He was asking me questions about this pedestrian–car hit-and-run accident, and I could not answer him. He had a little notebook and pen to write with, but I was not any help describing the type of car it was or any description of the man driving the car. The officer just looked at my parents and shook his head. Then he left. When my dad carried me out to the car, the neighbors stood in their front yard and had concerned faces as they looked at me. When there's an accident, people always want to watch.

My parents took me to a clinic nearby where the doctor on duty looked me over and washed my scraped-up knees and hands. He noticed my fat swollen lips. I told my parents that I was okay with no broken bones. He cleaned by wounds again, bandaged my skinned knees, and cleaned the blood off my little hands. Then, he must have said something to my parents because they decided to take me out to a restaurant to get something to eat and the to the movies afterward, which really did make me happy. I guess it was in an attempt to make me forget about what happened.

I have often thought about the little girl in me who was so scared and traumatized. For a while, these incidents changed me from who I was supposed to be but would soon have a turnaround point in my life. What would I say to that little girl in me? The enemy meant harm by afflicting me in my later years with PTSD that manifested in panic attacks and anxiety, but I would soon get set free. Those chains that formerly bound me became a testimony, bringing glory to God in the highest. He always provides a way out.

> *"There hath no temptation taken you but such as is common to man: but God is faithful, who will not suffer you to be tempted above that ye are ale; but will with the temptation also make a way to escape, that ye may be able to bear it." (1 Corinthians 10:13, KJV)*

I really believe that if I had not suffered the pain then, my joy wouldn't have been as full as it is today because I learned how my Father God is so faithful. He is such a big awesome God that words can't adequately describe completely all that He is. That's why, at times, I just sit here in tears because I am filled to fullness, and all the answered prayers are a testimony of how real our God is.

Later, my family and I moved to Seattle, and I thought it was great because I got to have a room to share with my older sister. This was a big five-bedroom house we were to rent over the next several years. We children started going to a new school. It was new and exciting at first, but when I looked all around me, there were not any other children who looked like me. The entire class was filled with only white students, and I felt a little shy making friends. I was the only person of color present in my class. Soon some of the kids were calling me racist names like, "Hey, brownie." They also called me "four eyes" because I wore glasses. I was not ashamed of until that point, but I kept wearing my glasses, nonetheless.

There was one summer when my best friend Kris and I went to the neighbor's house, which was on the other side of her house, because the little girl invited us to go swimming in her little pool in her backyard. So I put on a swimsuit and grabbed my towel. The three of us were having a great time in the summer sun, when one her parents called her to come into her house, so she left us to see what they wanted. When she came back to us, her head hung low, and then she sadly looked at me and said, "You have to go home."

I asked, "You mean me?"

Hesitantly, she nodded her head. I left, not knowing why I had to leave, but later on I learned from my friend that it was because of my skin color. I was ashamed of myself at that moment and wished that I were white because then the kids would not make fun of me at school. I didn't want to be so different that I would be asked to get out of someone's pool, as if I were a contaminant.

I would also hear from my siblings about the racial differences in the neighborhood. There were kids who could not play with us and who stayed away. My siblings would get into physical altercations with kids on our playground. The teacher at my school was always mean to me. I would get scolded for things that I didn't know was wrong to do. I was embarrassed and often felt shamed.

This woman lived around the corner from my friend Shelly's house, and I would pass by her house to take a short-cut through the fence. I had done this several times, and I thought it was harmless. One day at school after recess, we all lined up to go back to our class as we normally did, but this time, that mean playground teacher motioned for me to get out of line and step aside so she could speak to me. I was scared thinking, *What did I do?* She scolded me, shaking her finger in my face, saying, "You stop going near my yard! You stay off my property!"

Her look was meant to intimidate me. That ordeal really shook me and completely ruined my day. When I got home from school, I told my mom what had happened, and she was upset by it too. My dad worked the graveyard shift at the truck stop in another nearby city, and when he heard about it the next day, he was fuming mad and protective like I'd never seen him before.

Anyone who mistreated me had to answer to my dad. He always came to my defenses. Early the next day, he went straight to the school and asked to speak to the principal, and the secretary attempted to let the principal know that my dad wanted to talk to him, but he tried to refuse my dad's request by saying he was busy.

My dad then said, "I'm not leaving until I speak to him!"

By this time, my dad was even more angered. He let the principal know what the playground teacher said to me. He defended me by letting them know that no one would ever mistreat his daughter. After that, the principal very firmly told the secretary to get that playground teacher in the office. I believe she was reprimanded for her actions toward me. My parents told me to take the long way to my friend's house and never to step foot on her property, which I never did.

I have learned from these incidents now as I look back that nothing that came against me—whether it be an accident or mistreatment due to skin color—would ever change the plan that God had for my life.

> *"No weapon formed against thee shall prosper: and every tongue that shall rise against thee in judgment thou shalt condemn. This is the heritage of the servants of the Lord, and their righteousness is of me, saith the Lord." (Isaiah 54:17 KJV)*

In living life for God, there are many sufferings that we go through, but nonetheless our God reigns.

> *"Let the heavens rejoice, and let the earth be glad; let them say among the nations, 'The Lord reigns.'" (1 Chronicles 16:31, NIV)*

In all that we go through, no matter how painful, we can be encouraged that Christ Jesus suffered so much more for our sake. He made it through, and so can we.

> *"I have told you these things, so that in me you may have peace. In this world you will have trouble. But take heart! I have overcome the world." (John 16:33, NIV)*

Praise God we are overcomers.

> *"And they overcame him by the blood of the Lamb, and by the word of their testimony; and they loved not their lives unto death." (Revelation 12:11, KJV)*

There is one more accident to speak of to tell the whole story of my victory and deliverance. When my family and I relocated to Seattle I had just learned to ride a bike, so I must have been around seven years old. The neighborhood kids and I decided to take a ride around the block. I did not have a bike of my own, so they had me borrow my friend's older brother's bike, which was too big, but I thought I could manage. When we turned down this street I had never been before, I started to gain too much momentum, but I held on firmly to the handlebars. However, at the end of this street was a curb and then an embankment that dropped down about twenty feet to the street below.

I could not stop, so when my bike hit the curb, over I went with the bike, tumbling and falling down bushes and over debris that scraped my back. There were people in the cars and passersby that saw it all unfold. I got up and felt dazed and disheveled. My friends told me to just walk home, and they would take the mangled-up bike back to the neighbor's house. I went home and when my mother saw me with dirty clothes and hair awry, she was a little concerned to say the least. She checked my body over and discovered my back had bloody skid marks, so she took off my clothes and had me soak in a warm tub. She did not take me to the doctor. If it were something more serious, she would have, but having nine of us children, she knew what home remedies to use.

Still, God was in control. When He chooses us, there is not anything that can take us out. His will for our lives will always prevail.

> *"He brought me up also out of a horrible pit, out of the miry clay, and set my feet upon a rock, and established my goings." (Psalm 40:2, KJV)*

I did not write this book so that people would have pity on me but for the reason of giving testimony of my Savior God in all His glory. I have overcome the enemy. Giving testimony about what God has done is spiritual warfare in our race. We have what it takes for defeat and victory. Hallelujah!

LIFE EVENTS

I experienced sexual incest at an early age from an older sibling. It began from the time we lived in a small two-bedroom house in Eastern Washington. Since all of us children slept together all in a row on the living room floor, one could see how this might have happened. The decision to place brothers and sisters next to each other was out of necessity. During the night, I would get woken up by unwanted fondling and touching, but I was not strong enough to push this older sibling off me.

When we moved to Seattle, the incest continued there for a while but less often. My older siblings got their own rooms. I started sleep walking, which was probably triggered by the stress of the incest. I was told that I would wake, walk around the house up and down the staircase, and turn off and on the lights. My family members would simply put me back to bed and that was that. I never remembered any of these things the next day. I also wet the bed until about age nine. During one of these sleep-walking incidents, I guess I stumbled into the room at the foot of the stairs that belonged to the sibling who was molesting me.

All I remember is waking up, standing outside in the hallway of this room with my mom scolding me. She was holding a wire coat hanger. I kept nodding off back to sleep, and she began belittling me with, "What are you doing in there, you dirty nasty girl?" I did not respond because I didn't remember, so she shouted, "Answer me!" She then told me to go back to bed. From that point on, I learned that I was shameful.

Even earlier than this was the fact that when my grandfather was babysitting my little brother and me, he was also sexually touching me in the back seat of the car while my grandmother was in the store. I was left in the back seat long enough for this unwanted fondling to happen. Again, I never told anyone.

Not only did sexual abuse happen from this sibling but physical abuse at his hands as well. There was one time when the trash was burned out back in a metal burn barrel, and my older brother thought it would be funny to tease me and scare me by pretending to put me in that burning trash can. He lifted me to put me inside of it, and as I was kicking and screaming, my leg hit the edge of that metal container and burned me. I still have that dark burn scar on the back of my leg.

Another time when we were playing in the basement of that big white house, this same older sibling had a knife in his hand. He was high on marijuana, and he came behind me to scare me with the knife. I jumped to get away and got cut, causing some bleeding. I ran upstairs to let my mother know what he had done, but she just checked the wound cut, then told me to stay away from him. He was older at this point, and my parents were having uncontrollable teenage rebellion issues with two of my older brothers.

Incoming phone calls were especially important, so if me or my older sister answered the phone, he would punch us, sometimes leaving bruising on us. By this time, the impact of the abuse left its mark because I had low self-esteem. When I look at photos of myself, I can see that I was an attractive young girl, but I really did not have a healthy self-image.

I did not know it back then, but God was at work behind the scenes, lining things up, making things happen. He was teaching that I was not to be shamed, but He was also waiting for me to come to Him. He brought Isaiah 54 to my attention.

> *"Fear not; for thou shalt not be ashamed: neither be thou confounded; for thou shalt not be put to shame: for thou shalt forget the shame of thy youth." (Isaiah 54:4, KJV)*

I also was unaware of the restoration my God was preparing for me, because much of my youth was consumed with sexual and physical abuse and other events designed to take me out. God's promises were coming to me through books I would read or sermons I heard. Father God used different ways of speaking to me.

> *"And I will restore to you the years that the locust hath eaten, the cankerworm, and the caterpillar, and the palmerworm, my great army which I sent among you." (Joel 2:25, KJV)*

TEEN PREGNANCY

God did do a great work in my young life after the salvation of our household, mainly my parents and those of us children remaining at home. We attended a Bible-based Christian Church every Sunday and sometimes on Wednesdays as well. At the local junior high, I was in the 100-Mile Club, with my name engraved on a plaque displayed in the hallway. I was athletic. In our seventh-grade gym class, out of thirty kids, me and a boy were the only ones who could climb a rope to the ceiling, ring the bell, and then climb back down. This was where I discovered that I took after my mom and was afraid of heights, because coming back down was more labor intensive, and I was freaking out inside but I did it afraid.

Later, I attended a private Christian school, and my grades improved. I got certificates and won student body secretary. It was a small school. I helped us win victories at volleyball games and flag football games against the other local Christian schools. There was one time when I practically won the entire volleyball game by finding a weak spot, which was a girl who didn't know how to play.

I would serve the ball straight to her, and sometimes she would catch the ball, while other times I served directly to her, and she would swing aimlessly at the ball. I just kept up the same technique until that game was over and we won that set. The other team complained and said it is not fair. The pastor of that church was there, and he thought it was so hilarious. He could not stop laughing. I had a good time. It was a good memory. I had all these accomplishments, so there were high expectations of me to go on and do well with a bright future.

Things were going well, but as I turned fifteen, things changed when I met and fell in love with my first boyfriend. There were red flags I ignored about his abusive behavior seen by other people, and I was embarrassed but remained with him. I did not know how to set healthy boundaries, or that I was even worthy of doing such proactiveness. We were together two years when I learned I was pregnant.

I was four months along in my pregnancy when I first went to the doctor and learned of the life-altering event. My parents met with the pastor of our church, they discussed our situation, and said it would be best if they just let us get married. We both dropped out of high school. At six months along, and seventeen years old, we got married in a small ceremony at his parents' house with a big reception at the local church hall. We were given a nice reception with lots of wedding presents, which we didn't expect.

I believe due to the boundaries being crossed sexually at a young age, I did not know how to set boundaries for myself, and I didn't think I was valuable enough to be highly regarded. I had some sex education in sixth-grade public school. I tried to ask my mom questions, which made her very uneasy, and she responded, "You just never mind."

I did not know much of male behavior because we never had those conversations. I was never taught that I should wait until marriage because that is how special I am. This is a gift you give to your husband. She would rather that we just never had sex at all, which was not the case when it came to me. Sex was already introduced to me at an early age. I learned it was dirty and that I should be ashamed of myself.

I dropped out of high school temporarily until after our baby was born. We named her Melissa Ann, and she came with a head full of dark hair. She was a beauty, and I fell in love with her as well as with being a mom. All the motherly instincts kicked in, and I did well. I went back to school when she was eight months old and graduated only a year later because I had a lot of credits from working ahead. I was ranked forth out of a class of eighty students. I did not realize this until later after looking at my transcripts.

DOMESTIC VIOLENCE

I was an incredibly young fertile mother, so I got pregnant again. My husband did not have a good-paying job. His dad, my father in-law, who was a retired army veteran asked my husband at that time what he planned to do with a second baby on the way. When he responded "I don't know," my father in-law decided that wasn't an acceptable answer, so he immediately took him to the local army recruiters and made him enlist in the army. Since my husband at that time did not finish high school—nor ever went back—his scores on the entrance exam were exceptionally low. He did not qualify for other jobs that he would have preferred, so the only option was infantry. Infantry is often on the frontlines during war times.

I was now an army wife for the next ten years. The marriage was good in the beginning. However, I often had a feeling I was resented because of the sudden responsibility that was now placed on my young husband. I could not work because I was a young mother. I liked being a stay-at-home mom. I see photos of myself, and I was always busy, changing diapers and potty training the next baby. Then just as my husband found out he had orders to go to Germany, I found out I was pregnant with our third child. I felt like a single mom and perhaps resentful as well during the hard times. My husband came home, and he was able to meet the new baby for the first time. She was a year old by this time. We were then stationed in Texas for one year.

Serving in the army in infantry was incredibly stressful on the marriage especially when we were overseas. He was gone most of the time out in field duty. Sometimes weeks, other times months. When he was stationed in Germany with us, me and the kids felt isolated. There were only few places we could go. We went to the commissary to get groceries; the Stars and Stripes bookstore, where we could get the latest magazines and newspapers; and the PX, where we could shop for clothes toys, and household items.

We did try to learn German, and the girls learned some in school. I was amused at their attempts. It was cute. Occasionally we would shop on the German economy, but the American dollar was not at a high rate compared to the deutsche mark. Where we lived there were these high-rise apartment buildings all grouped together, and Germans knew these were where the Americans lived.

Every city in Germany has its own castle because of the history of war times. Oftentimes, I would go by myself on a bike ride along this trail, and I could see the many backyards of German people, who loved growing gardens and spending time outdoors.

There was a little bridge I would ride over, passing over a little babbling brook. Once I even saw a small heard of sheep. I had to stop and wait for them to pass. I will always remember this scenic part of Germany.

Germans love to celebrate, so this was the first that I learned of Octoberfest, where there is a carnival and a beer tent. This was great to be a part of. However, the drinking is what I regret participating in. I did not drink before I went overseas, but I was encouraged by my husband and the other wives. I did not find a good church to belong to because there was only a Catholic and a Baptist church, and we did not belong to either one. I was a Christian, who had backslid at this point. I lost focus of life's direction and really felt that I could not find God there in my life. This was where I really was lost and gave into the peer pressure to do what everyone else was doing, regrettably. It was at one of these events where I was physically abused by my husband.

There was a boxing ring there inside of the beer tent, and I needed to use the bathroom, so I let my husband know that I would be right back. But when I came back, in his drunken state, he did not know where I was so it angered him. I had just reentered the tent, and when he saw me, he began charging at me physically. When he got to me, he grabbed my shirt and threw me against the food trailer.

One of the military police saw the whole thing and radioed for help. I tried to get free from his grasp. My shirt was still in his hand, and everyone could see my exposed bra. I was embarrassed and traumatized by the whole ordeal. Nothing happened to my husband. The military protects their own, and even though he had just abused me, leaving bruises on both of my upper arms, I was told I could go to the MP office and file a report. I did not do it because he would get into trouble from his company commander and not get promoted, and they would punish him by citing him and taking money out of his pay.

The second event of domestic violence that happened in our time in Germany was witnessed by two of my young children, and again, it did involve drinking on his part. It was to be our eight-year anniversary, and we had planned to go out for dinner alone, so I arranged for a sitter to come take care of the kids. My husband had been at a BBQ all day, which had a lot of alcohol; I was not aware of that until afterward.

When he came home in the evening very intoxicated, I sent the babysitter home because there was no way we were going anywhere with him as drunk as he was. This angered him a lot, and he told me to go to the bedroom. I thought he just wanted to talk, but he just said, "Okay come here," and he threw me on the bed.

He then said, "I'm so sick and tired of you."

Then he got on top of me and started to choke me. When I looked into his eyes, he looked like someone I did not know; he had so much hatred. I was gasping for air trying to breathe, and that was when the girls heard the commotion and came to check. They both were screaming and ran across the hall to get the neighbors for help.

By this time, I had scratched his face, and the shock of that made him stop. When the neighbor came in, he was completely off me. This time, again, no police were summoned. The neighbor, who was also in the military, just talked to him about never putting his hands on his wife. The wife of the neighbor tried her best to calm me down. She gave me a glass of water. This couple never made mention of this event again. They kept it to themselves. Even when they would see us out in public, we all carried on like nothing ever happened.

I was so shocked and scared by what had happened that I was in disbelief. I just sat there stunned and did not know what to do with the kids. I just told them to please get into bed. My husband left that night in a taxi. While he was gone, the only thing I could think of for comfort was reaching out in a long-distance call to the States to my parents. I told them both what had happened. They listened quietly. My dad stayed silent, and my mom cried. They did not have any advice really. They just told me to take care of myself, that they loved me, and we said our goodbyes.

This time, I did call his company barracks, and spoke to a soldier. "My husband came home from the company barbecue and was abusive to me."

He gave me the phone number to the commanding officer. I called that number and made a complaint. When my husband went back to work, he told me the commanding officer called him into his office and told him he should have better control over his family matters because he did not want to be bothered on his off time ever again. He also took note of the scratch mark on his face, as did his comrades, which was an offense wound from me fighting back for my life.

He came back a few hours later sober, very apologetic, and he had bought some food as a means to apologize. I could not eat because my throat and neck were injured from the choking. I could not swallow, even though I was hungry. There was a clicking sound whenever I swallowed. I did not know what was wrong with me, but I did not go to the doctor or tell anyone. I was so scared and alone.

My husband asked why I could not swallow food, and when I reminded him of the choking incident, he did not remember because of the alcohol. I asked, "Then why are you apologizing?"

He said it was because we were arguing. I just began sobbing, and he could not comfort me. I was afraid and distrustful of him from that point on. I did not feel any togetherness any longer; I was in survival mode and staying in the marriage for the sake of the kids. To this day, there is an old healed-over bone on the front right side that is visible on X-rays from when I was last injured from a neck sprain. The technician asked me if I ever broke my neck before, and I said that I had not but that I was in a car accident. I will never know if it was from that abuse or not.

I like watching medical shows on TV, especially *Dr. G: Medical Examiner* who performs autopsies. In one of her shows, she mentioned that the hyoid bone in the front of the neck is a bone that is an exceedingly difficult bone to break, and it is what she looks for in someone who is strangulated to death.

This information kind of startled and made me wonder if that was what happened to me; I shall never know for certain. What I do know for sure is that I became tolerant of abusive behavior.

What is more disheartening is that this abuse spilled over to my middle daughter, who was experiencing similar signs as I had in my youth. My husband not handle it well and was abusive to her with name calling and threatening to leave and never come back. I am guilty of not stepping in and taking up for her. We argued in private over the matter, but my daughter did not know; she just felt unprotected by me, and for that, I have deep regret. I was worried about my own safety and not her emotional health. Today, my adult daughter hurts over this, and all I can say to her is, "I was wrong. Please forgive me. I love you with all my heart."

After being abused for several years when I was younger, even though they were isolated incidents that did not occur all that often, I began to fight back physically. Two of my siblings witnessed this behavior from me. They were shocked because they had never seen me act out this way. Afterward, we talked, and I explained what I had been through. They partly understood, but this brother explained he could never tolerate any behavior like this around his family—not in his house and certainly not around his children.

I apologized to my husband, and me fighting back did not happen again until I started to go through our divorce. There was a physical altercation between the husband, the new girlfriend, and me. In retrospect, it looked like something out of *The Jerry Springer Show*; there was a lot of hair pulling, and I ending up on the ground. I do regret that happening, but he was my husband for seventeen years. That was a deep hurt, and my reaction was as a result of that.

It is a little comical to think of now. However, I learned from that experience. If a man wants to leave you for another woman and for drug use, then let him go. If you stay, you and your kids will be simply surviving, as I did. I made it through stronger and wiser, as well as closer to God than I will ever be. My ex is not fine. He has suffered heart ailments due to poor choices he made in his life, and doctors have said that he does not have long to live. I will have to suffer that loss with four of my adult children when the time comes and be there with them. I also believe in a God of restoration and healing. I also believe when God does take the children's dad home that he will go ahead of me. I know his heart is right with God because we had a conversation about that.

The last time he was in the hospital with an ailment and all of us were in his room together, I asked him if we could all gather around him to pray, and he agreed. So, the Holy Spirit directed me how to pray for him. I thought that I was supposed to pray for him to rededicate his life back to God, but this was not the case at all. God let me know that, so my prayer changed direction. Our prayer time felt the same as when we both were teenagers praying in church together. I prayed that his heart beats with the rhythm of life and functions in the perfection it was created to function, that the Lord God will give him sweet sleep, and that He would assign angels to camp around his room.

Also, I prayed that the Lord God give the medical staff wisdom and knowledge in caring for the father of my four children. When I spoke those words, my Father God was pleased, and I felt that a healing presence was there not only for my ex and his healing but for my adult kids there. There were many tears shed in that hospital room. I was able to give my ex a very meaningful hug, and he hugged me back. When I let go of him, I looked over at my eldest daughter, our firstborn. She was deeply moved and getting healed of hurt. Glory to God! My daughter posted something positive on Facebook about our visit; she thanked me openly about bringing her there and respecting their dad. I replied, "Moms should always respect their baby's dad."

CHAPTER SIX

REGAINING YOUR GROUND

GETTING UP

After getting knocked down in running your race of life, and something like divorce happens, you have no other choice but to get back up. When you are raising four children on your own you cannot just stay in bed and not face reality. The real world does not function that way. As I mentioned in a previous chapter, I wanted to stay in bed for weeks and just cry, but I eventually had to go see my family doctor. I let her know that I was going through a separation.

I could not eat or sleep well. I lost twenty pounds just like that. She had a tear in her eye seeing me this way, and she reluctantly got out her prescription pad and started me on an antidepressant. For the first time in my life, I was classified as clinically depressed and taking a prescription pill daily, but I had to take care of myself no matter the stigma related to depression. I could not have the mindset that I was following my sister, mother, or my grandmother in being mentally ill.

I clearly remember getting some health information from the state of Washington regarding mental illness. It gave a rough estimate on how many thousands of Americans suffer with mental illness, that it was not something to be ashamed of, and to seek treatment when needed. I thought, *Am I mentally ill? This cannot possibly be happening to me.* I believe a fear set into myself thinking that I was not normal. I went to the Word of God and listened to what God says I am.

> *"Let this mind be in you which was also in Christ Jesus." (Philippians 2:5, NIV)*

> *"So, God created man in His own image; in the image of God He created him." (Genesis 1:27, NIV)*

I no longer thought of myself as a mentally ill person, but the fight against depression continued. I became a worshipper, and demons had to flee at the name of Jesus. No other name but the name of Jesus. The lyrics to the song "Even Louder" says: a song on the Christian radio station with, "The bigger the depression hits, the louder my praises gets."[4]

The children and I sought help with family counseling, and it did help for a while. Our faith in God and a good counselor helped us get through some very tough times. My oldest daughter attempted suicide, and that was when I first began to experience chest pain that turned out to be panic attacks. I needed more medicine for that as well. I was on state assistance for the children's medical insurance, and since I was now having problems with attendance and being late for work, the state had me take a psychological exam.

I was diagnosed with depression, PTSD, and ADD. The adult ADD I think I had since I was a child because I was held back in the second grade. I felt like I flunked second grade, but my family and teachers were nice to me about it. However, as an adult, the symptoms of ADD can be a challenge to deal with. I was not able to focus or finish projects, and I started running late because I was getting distracted.

The medication for the ADD kept me on track during the day, and I got things accomplished, but then at night, I had to take medication for sleep. After a few years, I began getting heart palpitations, so the doctor had me stop. He upset about me getting diagnosed with ADD because he disagreed with that diagnosis. He said I seemed like a bright young woman. He wrote a letter to the facility where I was getting counseling.

After six sessions with that counselor, she said I did not need to see her any longer. She stated that perhaps my inability to concentrate and focus could be sleep apnea with the same symptoms. She recommended I take a sleep study to rule out and that she was releasing me.

Even after getting back up from being knocked down, you can still remain strong and steady. You may get hit from the left unexpectantly and then from the right with continued hardships, which are a part of life. But you will notice that once you recover and regain your stance, there's a quickening and a repositioning that you take hold of in your strengthening. Your core is stronger now.

As you look to God for the next step and seek His wisdom on what to do next, you become keener and more aware of the enemy's tactics and strategies. There seems to be a pattern of the way the attacks come at you. They may come at you one after another out of nowhere. Then for a while they may fade out, but you should always be prepared because the next attack can come without warning or pattern of the last attack. And you should never consider yourself as being *under attack*, but *on the attack* as a soldier in God's army, fully equipped with strength and discernment.

> *"God's Word is quick, and powerful, and sharper than any two-edged sword, piercing even to the dividing asunder of soul and spirit, and of the joints and marrow, and is a discerner of the thoughts and intents of the heart." (Hebrews 4:12, KJV)*

It should come as no surprise that the tactics the devil uses are intended to get us down. The ones we love the most can be used to hurt us with words that cut like a knife. You can say it out loud, if need be: "I don't receive that." Or sometimes it is better to not say anything at all.

> *"A gentle answer turns away wrath, but a harsh word stirs up anger. The tongue of the wise adorns knowledge, but the mouth of the fool gushes folly. The eyes of the Lord are everywhere, keeping watch on the wicked and the good." (Proverbs 15:1–3, NIV)*

When you do the right thing and don't say anything, then their words will go back to them, and their conscience is what's left for them to deal with, which is not pleasant.

> *"The eyes of the Lord are in every place, watching the evil and the good." (Proverbs 25:22, KJV)*

Finally, after raising up with a stronger core, you can be certain that you are now even stronger than before because you survived, and you learned how faithful God is. You have now a pearl of wisdom, and you are now even closer to finishing the race that is only yours to run.

SINGLE PARENTHOOD

In the aftermath of divorce with children—with the other parent not involved in coparenting—came single parenthood. I was shocked that the man I married left me alone to raise his four children. I never wanted to be labeled as a divorced person, even though I was the one who had to pay for and file the divorce papers. I hired a lawyer to do this for me, since it involved property and custody of children. I felt that if I were abandoned by my husband, then I needed to file for divorce because it would then feel like a lingering open wound. With papers, there's proactiveness and a finality. That strength came from my faith in God.

It wasn't fun, but I often had to put my pride aside and stand in lines at the food bank, clothing bank, or at Christmastime in a longer line for presents for the kids. There were many times when we were put on a list for needy families from the kids' school, and they blessed us with gifts, as did our church with a dinner and all. This was how God provided. He used resources to meet our needs. I often cried tears of joy because God came through for us again. Through these hard times, I learned that He is my All-Sufficient Savior.

> *"And he said unto me, My grace is sufficient for thee: for my strength is made is made perfect in weakness." (2 Corinthians 12:9a, KJV)*

Part of getting through these situations was dealing with the resentment and anger I was feeling inside. I went to a women's anger management group, and we talked about passive-aggressive anger. The leader of the group called my name out loud when it was my turn to share. I didn't say what one would normally assume: "Hello, my name is Annette, and I am angry."

I opened my mouth, and there was such deep hurt and pride that I did not want to admit defeat. So, I cried openly. The leader of the group asked if anyone had words of support for Annette. She explained that my ex left me and four children for another woman and drug life. I shared with this group of women, and I broke down and cried in front of everyone. But then to my surprise, we bonded.

I had just injured my back and was off work for six weeks and had just finished rehabilitation. They thought I meant rehab as if I used drugs or alcohol. The process was grueling, and I was so tired and in pain. When someone asked me how I was doing, all I could do was cry, but it felt good. I shared that through my faith in God I was able to forgive my ex. One of the women was totally taken aback by what I shared, and she asked blatantly, "Who told you, you had to forgive him?"

I said, "Nobody but it's my choice not to hold on to the resentment and bitterness, so for my well-being, in order to let go I had to forgive."

> *"For if ye forgive men their trespasses, your heavenly Father will also forgive you; But if ye forgive not men their trespasses, neither will your Father forgive your trespasses." (Matthew 6:14–15, KJV)*

In running my race in life. and going through a painful divorce, I believe forgiveness was the best gift I could ever give to myself. There may continue to be new hurts that arise from new situations, but I still choose forgiveness, and as time goes by, the easier it has gotten. God's Word has something to say about this act of obedience.

> *"And Samuel said…to obey is better than sacrifice." (1 Samuel 15:22, KJV)*

In knowing that providing for my children was completely now my responsibility, I filed the necessary legal paperwork for child support, but I knew I would never see anything come of it, so I didn't make it a part of my financial planning. I decided that it was time to pursue my dream of becoming a registered nurse. I was a housekeeper in a hospital setting, and I worked at various jobs in the medical field. Still, becoming a nurse was my choice. So, I went to the local community college and made an appointment to meet up with a counselor. I filled out the paperwork for financial aid, and when I got approved, I then was able to enroll as a student. I was so excited, but I started out slow. I began by taking a computer class on the weekend before my first class in Psychology 100. I was still working full time at the hospital as a housekeeper.

KEEPING EMPLOYMENT

The first year was hard being a student full time and working full time. I had to depend on one of the older children to look after my son who was only three years of age when his dad and I split up. I was never home and could never get him into anything extracurricular because I was not there to pick him up or take him there. I had tremendous guilt over that much of the time. Sometimes my youngest would get sick, and I would have to leave work to pick him up from daycare and miss a class. My job suffered from either being tardy or having to call in. I started having migraine headaches frequently.

My doctor tried me on various medications for the depression, anxiety, and headaches. The doctor told me these ailments were stress related and that I was going to have to find a balance in my life. I was not willing to give up just yet. I got help with the disability support at the college, and that helped for a while to get accommodations for my classes in case I missed a class or a test due to these headaches. By law, the instructor had to work with me. Most of my instructors were flexible and did work with me, but there was one who was not, and she was my breaking point. I did not see that I would pass this biology class, and that the instructor offered no support, so I decided to drop out of college. I told myself it was temporary.

Not long after dropping out of college, keeping my full-time job at the hospital continued to be a struggle, and my boss, who also was not supportive of me, was trying to find ways to get around the job accommodations for my chronic migraine headaches. I would have to leave work early or call in sick, or often I was late. When he found out that he could not avoid me, he'd negatively communicate with a handful of my coworkers about me and my attendance. They were his favorites, and there was tension created. It felt very much like emotional abuse. Later, when I no longer was working for him, the headaches went away, and a heavy weight was lifted off my shoulders like I had never experienced before.

Single parenting was weighing heavily on me. It was feeling as if everything that I'd been working so hard to keep together was about to bust at the seams at any given moment. I felt that I was going to lose everything, even my sanity. I could not afford to go crazy. Who would take care of the children? Sometimes, I even felt as if I were holding my breath or had dreams that I couldn't breathe. It always felt like I was forgetting to do something, or that I did not do it right or good enough. It was the enemy I was listening to in those years because he was trying to get to me while I was down.

> *"Be alert and of sober mind. Your enemy the devil prowls around like a roaring looking for someone to devour." (1 Peter 5:8, NIV)*

I heard the lie that no one would ever want me or love me now that I was alone with four children. I also could hear that I was now used merchandise, tossed aside.

> *"Ye are of your father the devil, and the lusts of your father ye will do. He was a murderer from the beginning, and abode not in the truth, because there is no truth in him. When he speaketh a lie, he speaketh of his own: for he is a liar, and the father of it." (John 8:44, KJV)*

There were other times when I did not pray and ask God for help because the enemy would remind me of how I was such an imperfect Christian, or not a Christian at all. There was always guilt that I did not pray enough or read my Bible enough or attend church regularly because of my weekend work schedule. I was in bondage for years because I could hear the negative voice over my shoulder, and I was agreeing with it instead of coming against it.

> *"And the great dragon was cast out, that old serpent, called the Devil, and Satan, which*

> *deceiveth the whole world: he was cast out into the earth, and his angels were cast out with him. And I heard a loud voice saying in heaven, Now is come salvation, and strength, and the kingdom of our God, and the power of his Christ: for the accuser of our brethren is cast down, which accused them before our God day and night. And they overcame him by the blood of the Lamb, and by the word of their testimony; and they loved not their lives unto death." (Revelation 12:9–11, KJV)*

Not walking in the truth led me to not knowing who I was in Christ, nor did I know I was in any possession of boldness or strength to conquer these mountains. What ultimately ended up happening is believing what my employer said would happen if one more occurrence took place with my attendance. They recommended that I turn in my resignation, or I would be terminated. I ended up giving them my two weeks' notice to quit. Then when I applied for unemployment, I was denied because I had quit my job. However, I appealed and won my case. The judge ruled in my favor because of my family situation. As a single parent, I was not guilty of any deliberate act of not following company policy or procedure willfully but rather due to extenuating circumstances. I was able to collect unemployment until I found another job.

I was doing the best I could with attempting to regain my ground after getting knocked down, and for a while it felt like I was defeated or that I had lost the battle. It was not over yet. I was very discouraged, and I could not see how everything would get better. Some well-meaning Christians would say something cliché that came from the Bible, such as, "Well, you know God will never give you more than you can handle." This was no comfort to me, but now that I look back on it, and I see what they meant to say, and I see in hindsight there was truth in it.

> *"There hath no temptation taken you, but such as is common to man: but God is faithful, who will not suffer you to be tempted above that ye are able; but will with the temptation also make a way to escape, that ye may be able to bear it." (1 Corinthians 10:13, KJV)*

I have learned through going through these hard times that God never promises to deliver us from any of it. Some of my prayers were not answered like I prayed for. He was always faithful. He was most definitely purifying me. The dross had to come out. He wants me to stand before Him pure and holy without blame. Today I am a woman with virtues, but it didn't come from what I was taught in my early years in Catechism in the Catholic school I attended in third-grade first communion, dressed in white with veil, hands folded and posed for our class photo.

> *"Consider carefully what you hear," he continued. "With the measure you use, it will be measured to you—and even more." (Mark 4:24, NIV)*

SELF-REFLECTION

- In your life's race, what situations or circumstances would you say you have personally come up against?
- How did you handle those setbacks? By yourself or with God's help?
- How did you regain your ground?
- What are your personal scriptures where the truth of God is louder than deception?

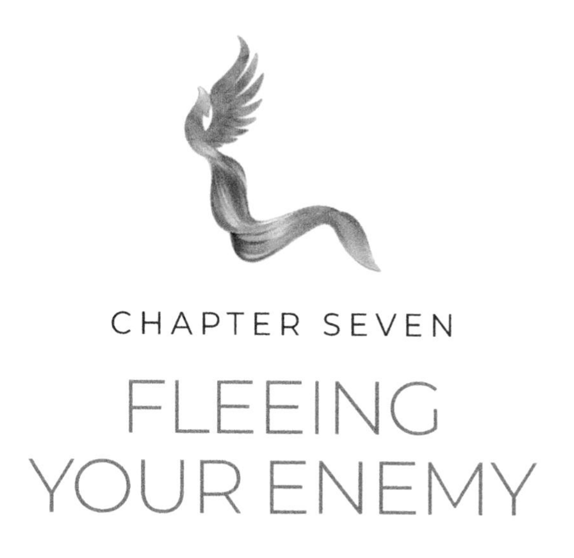

CHAPTER SEVEN

FLEEING YOUR ENEMY

SPIRITUAL WARFARE

After being single for several years, I got into a long-term relationship. We did not marry, but we do have a daughter together, Sofia. She was unplanned but known to God and definitely not a mistake. If it were not for her, I would be alone right now. She is the last child I am raising. Her father wanted to marry, but I did not because I knew he was not the right one. I knew I would be going through another divorce. He was also physically abusive to me and unfaithful many times in our time together.

Throughout this four-year relationship, I was still in bondage and believing the lies of the enemy. I would go to church but felt judgment from other Christians because I had a child and was not married. My self-esteem was at an all-time low. The depression made me feel like I had no way out. I was no longer drinking, but the restaurant bar was where I met Sofia's dad. That relationship ended in an awful way, and I ended up needing an order of protection against him and his two brothers from Mexico living in the area. They were threatening me because he was arrested and the thought it was all my fault.

As I write this chapter of this book, it is November 1, which is 11-1, and it can be considered a flip of Deuteronomy 1:11, which is a prosperity verse I learned well, going through the healing school and ordination with Joan Hunter.

> *"May the Lord God of your fathers make you a thousand times..." (Deuteronomy 1:11, NKJV)*

Joan posted on Facebook about this being a turnaround time for situations to change and for the Lord to bless you. She also shared John 11:1, which is the story of Lazarus being raised from the dead, which is that a situation will be turned around for the benefit of the people, that they would believe.

In the same regard, this part of my life was over, but it was a turning point in a good way. Things were about to change. Since I was no longer in a sinful relationship outside of marriage, I was now free and able to fully surrender to God. I turned away from sin and said yes to God. It was the best decision I ever made. I had been wanting to get out of that relationship for the last two years, but he would not let go of me, saying we needed to stay together because of Sofia. But no longer. I was free. When I went to church, I paid no attention to the judgment. I did not feel connected with this church, but I went anyway because I truly needed it. I kept going weekly, and whenever they had an altar call, I went forward because I always had some need. I was going through a dark time in my life, and I asked for prayer a lot. Unfortunately, sometimes a prayer request turned into gossip.

> *"Yea, though I walk through the valley of the shadow of death, I will fear no evil: for thou art with me; thy rod and thy staff they comfort me." (Psalm 23:4, KJV)*

The mobile home I was living began to have a lot of demonic spiritual activity, and I could not understand it because now I was fully completely serving God the best I could. I worked the graveyard shift, and sometimes when I was gone, the spirits would do things in my home to cause fear in the children. They would hear voices or see things move on their own. Coat hangers flew across the room. Lights were shut off and on. Doorknobs jiggled. This all began after my husband left, but it became more intense when I got serious in my walk with God. I told my family, and they thought because of all the hardship I experienced that I must be going crazy. I even questioned my own sanity because this spiritual warfare was now waking me up at night. My work hours changed, so I was on dayshift.

At my church, there was a couple who oversaw the prayer hotline. I called this couple many times, and I knew they were praying for me, fighting the fight, and I appreciated it. I could call them day or night. I would get woken up by these tormenting demon spirits. They would hover over me, shake my bed or move my pillow, or sit at the end of my bed. Sofia was a baby at this time, and when I commanded the enemy to flee, it would then hover over top of the baby and she would wake up screaming. After this happening to her several times, she got bold, and with her little chubby finger she pointed in the air and said, "NO!" and then went back to sleep.

I called the pastor of the church to please come pray over my home, but no one came. Then I heard that they were all going to pray and fast first, but they didn't receive anything from the Lord about me. After a while, word got around at church what was going on in my home, and people started to stay away from me. I felt very alone and afraid. Meanwhile, these attacks continued. I thought that I had done something to bring this on. I did not understand.

> *"Trust in the Lord with all thine heart; and lean not unto thine own understanding. In all ways acknowledge him, and he shall direct thy paths." (Proverbs 3:5–6, KJV)*

I would hear from sermons that the higher your you go with your Christian walk the deeper the spiritual warfare. Other sermons I would hear was that enemy recognizes your anointing, so the battle is stronger against you. In the beginning, Satan was a fallen angel. So, there are some things he has knowledge of.

I was encouraged in knowing that my future must be a great ministry because the enemy would not be working against me so strongly. A few other Christians I knew came and helped pray, anointing each doorway in my home with oil and pleading the blood of Jesus. Things would calm down for a while, then demonic activity continued even with my older brother living with us in the back bedroom. However, he was not protection for us, nor the man to be responsible for our family. The head of the household was gone, and we were now vulnerable for attack with no protection. I would walk around my house reading Psalm 91 aloud many times and praying cleansing prayers. The spirits would leave but then come back hours later.

What I really believe is that something happened on that property that Satan felt he had dominion over based on that activity of innocent bloodshed, suicide, witchcraft, or whatever occurred previously. When I sold that property and moved out, some activity did follow us to our next home, which was far from this place. By this time, I was spiritually stronger and well versed in knowing the authority I have as a believer. I was faster at taking authority and not being afraid. I was intolerant of being under attack and fully aware of the strategies and tactics the devil used, and I wasn't going to be defeated but walk in victory in Christ Jesus.

> *"Behold, I give unto you power to tread on serpents and scorpions, and over all the power of the enemy:*

> *and nothing shall by any means hurt you." (Luke 10:19, KJV)*

I also started to care less about what other people thought or said about me. I was now only going to be tuned in to what my Father God says about me.

> *"For I know the plans I have for you," declares the Lord, "plans to prosper you and not to harm you, plans to give you hope and a future," (Jeremiah 29:11, NIV)*

There was a something that happened to me at church after going forward for prayer at the beginning of the service. A woman prophetess came and laid hands on me, and the power of God came down on me so strong that I could not stand. It felt like a strong bolt of strong power. The people around me said they could feel it, so it was undeniable it was the hand of God.

While I was down, the church service carried on. The pastor preached the sermon, but I was still lying there. My Father God was talking to me, and I was nodding my head yes, and sometimes out loud I would say, "Uh hm." Because He said to me, "Remember that book you were reading that said that God watches over all the children of abuse all through their lives and sends angels along their way to make sure that they are all right?"

I said, "Yes," because I remembered.

Then He said, "Well, that's true because especially you, my love, I have watched over you, and I've been waiting for you all of this time."

The expression on my face revealed that that I had just heard the most beautiful thing in all my life. Kind of like taking your vows on your wedding day. Then he said comforting words to me because of the crying. He said, "Yes that hurt, didn't it?" I nodded my head yes again, and this time my lips and chin quivered, but then it was like He waved some more healing power all over me. It felt like electrical pulses all over. He said, "And that song, you loved that song." It was something only He and I knew.

I said to Him, "Please don't leave me," and I asked, "Can we always be close like this?"

He responded, "I will never leave you." Then He said, "Call My name."

> *"For whosoever shall call upon the name of the Lord shall be saved." (Romans 10:13, KJV)*
>
> *"Call to me and I will answer you, and will tell you great and hidden things that you have not known." (Jeremiah 33:3, ESV)*

My sister was there when this all took place, and she said it was about two hours I was out. She said it looked like I was praising Him and talking to Him. She asked a pastor who was there what was happening with me on the floor, and he said, "God is repairing her broken heart." A few people walked by me while I was on the floor, and they could feel the warmth and the electrical pulses when they put their hands over the top of me.

I heard a brother say, "Wow! I want some of that." Later, he asked me if God was talking to me at that moment, but I could not remember it all because at that moment I was really drunk in the Spirit. I could not even drive yet. I had to wait awhile. That brother also said that he would have given anything to have an experience like that.

Ever since that happened, I have been chasing God. He lets me catch Him. I cannot ever live without God in my life. My walk with Him is deeper, and He is always nearby. If I want to feel as close as I did that day, I just get some alone time with Him. When I first wake up in the morning with my coffee, I am in pursuit of Him. I read my Bible and start praying in the Spirit, and there He is with me. He never leaves me nor forsakes me. I can hear His voice clearer than ever.

Sometimes when a great idea pops in my head, that is my Father God talking to me. It is not my idea. Other times, He speaks to me in biblical terms, such as when He is reminding me of what the Word of God says about what I am talking to Him about. Still at other times, it is colloquial speech that I hear from Him. There are times when we are conversing without words, and it is more of an impression; even so, there is solidity without wavering.

More and more I've been getting visions and prophesies. When I was younger, I could never pay attention in school, and I was always daydreaming, but it would get me in trouble because the whole class knew what was going on. So when the teacher called on me, I did not have the answer. Little did I know then that the Lord would use that ability to give me visions of things He wanted to show me.

> *"And it shall come to pass afterward, that I will pour out my spirit upon all flesh; and your sons and your daughters shall prophesy, your old men shall dream dreams, your young men shall see visions." (Joel 2:28, KJV)*

I did find love again, and I remarried a second time. The marriage was good in the beginning, but after a few years, we began to have blended-family issues as predicted by the pastor and his wife, who warned us about this before we married. But my husband assured me he accepted my children, and he would provide for them and me. However, he became weary and unhappy about the situation. We got premarital counseling and marriage counseling.

He could never accept that he had an anger problem. He was attending because we had argued, and I reminded him of our need for help. He went for individual counseling as well but to no avail. He had suffered a head injury in his youth, so he had a disability. I knew of this beforehand, but I thought I could be the wife he needed. Through much of our relationship, I felt like his mother and he was a rebellious adolescent.

The tension grew worse at the knowledge that my fourteen-year-old son let me know that he was gay. This repulsed my new husband, and as soon as he told me of his hatred for my son, my love grew cold toward him. I was always protective of all my children, and since I was the only parent involved, the total responsibility was solely on me again as my husband withdrew his support for me and the children—even though he promised in counseling and in our marriage vows that he'd always be there.

He now had changed his mind but did not have the boldness to tell me, so he secretly began looking for another woman. He was on social media friend-requesting young women right and left. It was very hurtful and embarrassing because one of the women was my second cousin, and he did not know it until I showed him.

All through our five-year marriage, he acted out in anger, punching things and breaking items that were of sentimental value from our wedding presents because he knew it would hurt me. I would get panic attacks because of the fear it would set off in me from the domestic violence I witnessed as a young child. He knew of this but loved how it made him feel in control. That is the only explanation I could come up with, besides just wanting to be cruel and scare me. In our first year of marriage, I was in the hospital four times from chest pain. Each time, cardiac problems were ruled out. There were many red flags that should have been clear warnings not to marry him—and afterward as warnings to get out—but I married him anyway and remained. I continued to stay in the marriage because eventually I lost my on-call position at the local hospital from my poor attendance or being late.

One time after arguing, he took my wallet, car keys, and phone, and left to go to work with all my belongings. I believed he was trying to control me. The behavior was very scary. When he did this, I knew I was in a dangerous situation, but without a job, I did not know what to do. There was one occasion when we had argued before getting into the car to go work out at the YMCA, and so he drove very erratically. I told him in anger to stop driving this way, that the girls (daughter and granddaughter) were in the back seat. This made him even angrier, so when he turned the corner to go down another street, he acted like he was going to hit the oncoming car, but at the last moment he corrected his self.

I could not believe the cruelty and the inconsideration of the safety of me and the children. I most definitely felt like I was stuck with no way out and no job. At the time, the country was in an economic recession. I just sank deeper into depression again and sleeping a lot. For a while, that scene of us in the car headed toward the people in the other lane, and the looks on their faces, kept coming to me. I did not pray against it. A few times, the enemy tried to torment me with a nightmare of us driving toward a brick wall at high speed. I was the passenger with nothing to stop it from happening. My prayer life suffered due to lack of growth.

One Sunday, I had a bad headache, so I stayed home from church. I had no idea that he would take this as an opportunity to try to meet a woman, but that was exactly what took place. He kept this a secret for a while, but eventually, I found out. I confronted him with what I found, and he became really scared and didn't want to answer my questions. Then he said, "I'm leaving."

He quickly packed all his things and left. He left me for the woman he met at the mega church we were attending together as a married couple. I wanted to let the church know that this had happened at their church, so I wrote a letter to the church, but one of the associate pastors contacted me by phone. I told him that church is a great place for singles to meet, but my husband's behavior was totally inappropriate. They explained that unless he was serving the church in a position, they could not act on it and deal with him. With him just being a member, they said they didn't babysit.

They further explained that I'm more than welcome to continue attending but maybe just attend a different service time and avoid the area that he normally sits in. I believe I must have been looking for retribution, but none could be found in that moment. However, I would soon learn what the enemy meant for harm God was about turn around my situation for good. In order to move higher with God, sometimes He will take out people in your life that are hindering your walk with Him. In the time I was married to this man, I did not experience spiritual growth. Contrarily, I stayed stagnant. This is where the enemy wants us to be because you have no strength for spiritual warfare.

DIVORCED AGAIN

I was now free of a loveless marriage and free to serve God wholeheartedly. However, harder times were ahead. Over a three-year period, my youngest daughter and I experienced homelessness. We were not on the streets but stayed with relatives and friends. I lost sight of my dream job of working as an RN.

My daughter had some strong bonding during these trials. She changed schools several times and started to fall behind due to attendance as she lacked ambition to even try to do well.

God showed Himself to us during these difficulties. He always provided for us. We prayed together, and our mother–daughter relationship grew, allowing us to depend on one another even more. There were times when a provision would just appear out of nowhere, but we knew who it came from. When I reminded my daughter, "Look, didn't we just pray for that?" she would let out this little giggle when these God moments showed up, which was often because we totally relied on Him for everything. I went through different jobs and was tempted to lose hope, but that loss happened because He always had something better with higher wages. It continued until 2021, where I now have a full-time job with great benefits and pay higher than I asked for, but that's how God is, always exceeding our expectations.

CHANGE OF PERSPECTIVE

There are many different evangelists that I listen to. Joseph Prince preaches on grace, and I appreciate that. While Joyce Meyer teaches on how our minds are battlefields, and I've gleaned so much from that. I've heard from T. D. Jakes that we need to reposition ourselves, and that is great to learn. Casey Treat sermons teach on renewing the mind. I've really made good use of God's Word because this is one of the ways He speaks to me is through reading His Word or listening to a great sermon. When you renew your mind, it changes your perspective, and I believe that is very necessary.

> *"Do not be conformed to this world (this age), [fashioned after and adapted to its external, superficial accustoms], but be transformed (changed) by the[entire] renewal of your mind [by its new ideas and its new attitude], so that you may prove [for yourselves] what is the good and acceptable and perfect will of God, even the thing which is good and acceptable and perfect [in His sight for you]." (Romans 12:2, AMPC)*

When my thinking is renewed, I can get refocused, and with the guidance of the Holy Spirit, draw up a new plan. With God, plan B can be better than plan A. I am so thankful of how complete God's Word is.

> *"Remember not the former things, nor consider the things of old. Behold, I am doing a new thing; now it springs forth, do you not perceive it? I will make a way in the wilderness and rivers in the desert." (Isaiah 43:18–19, ESV)*

At that time, I began working again for the first time after three years of unemployment, and it was through a program at the college. I began taking a certified nurse's assistant course, so I could start working but continue with college course toward the licensed practical nurse to RN program.

My desire was that as I went through the process that my attitude would be conducive to my belief system. I wanted my internal dialogue to line up with the Word of God, so I looked closely at the fruits of the spirit, which can be challenging to keep in mind.

> *"But the fruit of the Spirit is love, joy, peace, longsuffering, gentleness, goodness, faith, meekness, temperance: against such there is no law." (Galatians 5:22–23, KJV)*

When you are walking in true fellowship, Father God the Spirit and the heart of God are alive and well within you, and you become more sensitive to what grieves the Holy Spirit. The choice of your speech, where you set your feet, and what you watch is affected, and people start to notice you. When they cuss, some will say, "Oh excuse me," and others may not, depending on whether they follow their conscience or ignore it.

PUTTING ON YOUR ARMOR

> *"Stand therefore, having your loins girt about with truth, and having on the breastplate of righteousness; And your feet shod with the preparation of the gospel of peace; Above all, taking the shield of faith, wherewith ye shall be able to quench all the fiery darts of the wicked. And take the helmet of salvation, and the sword of the Spirit, which is the word of God: Praying always with all prayer and supplication in the Spirit, and watching thereunto with all perseverance and supplication for all saints." (Ephesians 6:14–18, KJV)*

Nothing is more successful in spiritual warfare than having your full armor on. You are now prepared for battle. How else would you be able to stand firmly, knowing full well that you are well equipped?

SELF-REFLECTION

- What situations or circumstances are you aware of in your life today that you would consider spiritual warfare?
- Do you have a strategy?
- Are there ideas on which you need to change perspective?

CHAPTER EIGHT

FLY HIGHER

KNOWING THE LOVE OF A FATHER

Having the knowledge that my earthly father loved and cared for me the best that he knew how, and he was not perfect, was a great epiphany. I have not been a perfect mother by far. There have been faults in me for which I have had to apologize—for things I had done or said or not done or said. I may have not heard the words I needed from my dad, but I forgave him. I dearly loved him and felt his deep love for me. Even more so, I now know the love of my heavenly Father. How could I have not known before? I believe mainly because I was being deceived by the enemy, and for too long, I listened to the lies and the condemnation.

> *"There is therefore now no condemnation to them which are in Christ Jesus, who walk not after the flesh, but after the Spirit." (Romans 8:1, KJV)*

I now wanted to listen to the truth since I was no longer in the bondage of being deceived. My effort to research the scriptures on my worth and that I am loveable brought me up higher. I felt like a new person with a new bounce in my step. I felt confident when I spoke and a glimmer in my eyes when I smiled.

> *"But You, O Lord, are a shield for me, my glory, and the lifter of my head. With my voice I cry to the Lord, and He hears and answers me out of His holy hill. Selah [pause, and calmly think of that]!" (Psalm 3:3–4, AMPC)*

> *"Casting the whole of your cares [all your anxieties, all your worries, all your concerns, once and for all] on Him, for He cares for you affectionately and cares about you watchfully." (1 Peter 5:7, AMPC)*

> *"Because he has set his love upon Me, therefore will I deliver him; I will set him on high, because he knows and understands My name [has a personal knowledge of My mercy, love, and kindness—trusts and relies on Me, knowing I will never forsake him, no, never]. He shall call upon Me, and I will answer him; I will be with him in trouble, I will*

> *deliver him and honor him. With long life will I satisfy him and show him My salvation." (Psalm 91:14–16, AMPC)*

Before, I had an internal dialogue that said, *If my own family hurt me and was responsible for my brokenness, then who can I trust?* Now that I understood the love of a father, the walls of protection that I placed were coming down, and I could receive love and give love.

> *"A new heart also will I give you, and a new spirit will I put within you: and I will take away the stony heart out of your flesh, and will give you a heart of flesh." (Ezekiel 36:26, KJV)*

My Father God taught me that it is agape love when it's love He puts in us for others' benefit. Also, now that healing has taken place, I can read 1 Corinthians 13, which is the love chapter, and can fully appreciate it. I had memorized this chapter in my youth as part of the curriculum at the Christian school I attended.

> *vv. 1–2: "Though I speak with the tongues of men and of angels, and have not charity, I am become as sounding brass, or a tinkling cymbal. And though I have the gift of prophecy, and understand all mysteries, and all knowledge; and though I have all faith, so that I could remove mountains, and have not charity, I am nothing."*

vv. 5–8: "Doth not behave itself unseemly, seeketh not her own, is not easily provoked, thinketh no evil; rejoiceth not in iniquity, but rejoiceth in the truth; beareth all things, believeth all things, hopeth all things, endureth all things."

v. 13: "And now abideth faith, hope, charity, these three; but the greatest of these is charity."

(1 Corinthians 13, KJV)

HIGHER CALLING

As I have gotten older, I find myself in retrospect often or dreaming about when my children were young and in diapers. I awaken and realize they are now adult children, and this is my new normal. I find it healthy to acknowledge the past and look forward to the new and to whatever God has in store for me. With age comes an awareness that this is where my calling is now in action. Even in these golden years it is a higher calling without a doubt. It is as if He saved the best for last. Only God could do that. The time is now, and it could not have been no other than this time. I do know that despite all that has happened, God will use me. I am free and from sin and guilt.

"The Lord your God is gracious and merciful, and will not turn His face from you if you return to Him." (2 Chronicles 30:9, NKJV)

> *"Judge not, and you shall not be judged. Condemn not, and you shall not be condemned. Forgive, and you will be forgiven." (Luke 6:37, NKJV)*

> *"For he hath made him to be sin for us, who knew no sin; that we might be made the righteousness of God in him." (2 Corinthians 5:21, KJV)*

> *"As far as the east is from the west, so far hath he removed our transgressions from us." (Psalm 103:12, KJV)*

> *"And their sins and iniquities I will remember no more." (Hebrews 10:17, KJV)*

I once read a saying by Corrie Ten Boom that was so great. In picturing all of God's forgiven sins thrown into the sea, she said, "When we confess our sins, God casts them into the deepest ocean, gone forever… I believe God then places a sign out there that says No Fishing Allowed."[5]

Now I can really live the true meaning of forgiveness because all the doubt leaves me when I consider redemption. Because I have been forgiven of my sins and remembered no more, I've been redeemed by the blood of the Lamb. Now communion has a deeper meaning. Hallelujah! Christ was the sacrifice in exchange for redemption. Climbing higher and knowing my higher calling has now prompted me to act and investigate the process of getting ordained and getting some training on healing.

ORDINATION AND HEALING SCHOOL

Joan Hunter had been to a Pentecostal church on an Indian reservation about thirty miles away from where I am. Those services were so great. It was exactly what our church needed by witnessing healing and their faith to be strengthened. I was certainly blessed and encouraged. I was personally healed of carpal tunnel syndrome, which I suffered with for years being a housekeeper with the repetitive hand movements the job requires. Also sitting in the audience and receiving the overflow from someone else getting prayer for their knees was amazing. My knee got healed. Thank You, Lord!

She did a lot of teaching while she was there, and I soaked it all in. I was truly blessed by seeing a lot of people going forward for their healing, and the reactions of many were amazing. The anointing was so strong. God was so good to us. I agree with her that miracles happen. I bought an afghan with that phrase on it so that I could see it daily as it hung over the back of my couch. When she invited anyone interested in getting ordained and or attending the healing school, I got excited. I made it a plan to pursue this endeavor.

I knew I had a calling ever since I was a teenager, and the principal at my Christian school noticed this gift in me. I'm in my fifties, and now was the time. I kept hearing it deep inside my soul. I said, "Okay, Lord, will You provide?" I began putting money aside, and I asked the church I attended on Sunday afternoons if they would help with the finances, and they said yes.

People that I thought would be supportive of me going forward with this ordination and training were not, and I was taken aback, but nonetheless, I continued my pursuit. The woman in charge of the paperwork at Joan Hunter Ministries was very sympathetic and understanding. She explained that sometimes that happened because perhaps of someone's personal beliefs about women in ministry. She encouraged me to continue, and she even prayed with me over the phone. I had never experienced this professionalism, coupled with God's love and support. She was so patient, but at the same time, she kept me on track with the deadlines. It was incredibly challenging for me to stay on top of it all. There was a questionnaire to fill out that was in conjunction with several books with CDs, in which I had to complete by a certain time. This was extremely exciting when I first received them in the mail, but as the work started, I must confess, I was stressed. I turned to scripture when I needed to be strengthened, but also, I could feel God smiling down at me.

> *"Study to shew thyself approved unto God, a workman that needeth not to be ashamed, rightfully dividing the word of truth." (2 Timothy 2:15, KJV)*

I knew my diligence would pay off and that I could get through the first part of this training. It felt like being in one of my college classes, but only this time, the curriculum was the truth that lined up with my belief system. Glory to God!

The ordination was in Dallas, Texas. There was a nice lunch for us, and we all sat at tables of six. It was a little awkward at first getting to know people, but it felt like an orchestrated moment because we all began talking and eating at the same time. The women at the table, of course like myself, desired to get into ministry. As one by one they shared their own stories about themselves, their stories sounded like mine. This was not a coincidence but something lined up to happen at that time.

The woman to my left wanted to write her book about being a survivor of abuse. I learned that my story was similar to others. I would learn from sitting at this table that the time was now for me to write the book that I had been wanting to write for many years. The person who would help me along this journey was none other than one of Joan Hunter's daughters, Charity, who owns a publishing company and teaches an online class on how to write your story.

I leaped with joy inside that someone could help me do this. I could not believe it. I had no idea that God was making this all happen for me such as it was prophesied. He was waiting for the right time for this to take place, and the time was now. After all the pain, heartache, and the healing took place, it was possible to talk about what I had been through without getting a lump in my throat. No longer was there residual pain when I spoke about my past but a Holy Spirit countenance. Praise the Lord!

I like how God waited until much healing had happened in my soul before I met new people and felt safe sharing myself with others. Normally, I do not have a group of friends who I go and do lunch with. I prayed that God would send strong Christian women friendships my way, and now He has. Thank You, Jesus!

Networking is very key in ministry. This is my new normal, whereas before I would be isolated and not social due to previous bouts of depression, but praise God, I have been set free!

After the lunch on our first day, I sat next to a friendly woman, with whom I instantly felt amazingly comfortable and connected. She smiled or laughed with me during the session, and she let me know that she had written a new book. Again, I was amazed at how God was organizing the seating arrangements so that I would sit with her and be encouraged by her, because she was where I was had wanted to be, an author.

I purchased her book, she autographed it for me, and we took a picture together. I did not make any arrangements for dinner, so she invited me to go along with her new friend who drove a vehicle that sat seven. They both were from Texas and as friendly as could be. We really enjoyed our dinner together and took several pictures. We all shared what God was doing in our lives, and I believe the talk attracted the attention of others sitting around us. God was so good to give us such a good waitress. She treated us well. I had lived in Texas as a military wife, so I was fully enjoying that Texas hospitality. People there talk to you with terms of endearment, as if they had known you for years. Who would not love such affirmations?

The next sessions were teachings by Joan, and they were great testimonials of healings that took place, some right there in that church. She had us partner up, and we prayed for each other. God was doing a great work right there in our midst, and we were all in awe of the healing power of using our authority in

Jesus's name. People reacted emotionally, and there were lots of heartfelt outbursts of crying as they were getting delivered from bondages and physical healings. I prayed for a woman from Oregon who was a survivor of breast cancer.

For the first time, I asked God for a creational miracle, asking Him to grow new breast tissue, and she reacted tearfully because she felt the anointing so strongly. When we were praying for each other for height to be restored and the base of the skull to line up with the vertebrae in the spinal column, I felt my posture suddenly straighten up, and I felt taller. When I got back to the hotel room, I looked at myself in the mirror, and it appeared as if my double chin was reduced because of the miraculous correction of my posture. I took a selfie because I did not think I had ever seen myself look so joyful. I posted it on Facebook, and a good friend said that I looked so happy.

We had some great training with information in the lobby bookstore to help us further our ministries. On the third day, Joan's husband, Kelley, gave an excellent teaching on communion. Then there was a woman prophet who came and ministered and began calling on various individuals. She could see something in them. She spoke to each individual on what was going to happen or what was taking place right there, and it was extremely exciting.

She called Kelley to come up and join her, and I was just awestruck at how they both saw right into the spiritual ream and called things out. They both could see large angels lined up in the back. They were throwing beach balls around because they wanted us to enjoy this season in our lives. They talked about the angel of Houston being there as well as a glory cloud hovering over the church. They could see the roof of the church lifted off because it was opened to receive the ladder coming down from heaven with angels carrying vials of anointing oil, passports for those of us traveling, and luggage. They also said they could see a red carpet rolled out with a backdrop, such as they do in Hollywood for movie premieres. This event was even bigger and more important.

This woman at the end had us all line up because she had a personal word for each of us. When she got to me, she said, "When the word was given about the last will be first, that was for you," and I teared up. She continued, "You have a beautiful heart, you're very humble, and He's going to use you in a mighty way. You are going to travel with a team and do His work. You'll be used for work among your people." I was very moved emotionally and could not hold back the tears. There is nothing better than to witness a word coming straight from God through a vessel to me. I have been ministered to in this manner many times, and each time is precious. I always remember each word spoken, and when it comes into fruition, I celebrate.

There was a session where those of us who wanted to join the organization and have a covering could get pinned. Joan talked about the importance and the relevance of getting pinned. Those from the 50s era can relate to getting pinned. One by one, Joan pinned us. If she had a word for us, she would speak, but if not, she reminded us that she would not speak. When she got to me, she did not have a specific word for me, and I was okay with that because I was filled with the fullness of God. However, she did speak an impartation over me, and since then, I have felt a special anointing follow me. She said, "I impart to you the Spirit of apostleship to go forth and reach the nations." I was not sure exactly what that meant at that moment, but I felt a shift take place in the spiritual realm. My petitions in interceding for others took on a new priority. I sensed that my prayers had been answered quickly because He has been showing me that He is at work in those situations.

Not long ago, I was in a church service, and the guest speaker had us all come up front so he could speak a word over each of us. I entered in deep prayer while he spoke over others and enjoyed the Father's presence. When he got to me, he said, "You like to pray a lot don't you?"

I replied, "Yes I do."

He said, "And your prayers get answered quickly?"

Again, I said, "Yes."

He said, "I wish my prayers were answered like that."

I was humbled by that.

Then he asked, "Hey, could you pray for me and my ministry?"

I said sure.

He told me his name and the ministry and where abroad they were going to minister. He explained, "You pray for us, we get blessed, and you'll be a part of that."

I thought, *How awesome is that?* Wow.

As he passed by me, he remarked. "I've never met such a gentle spirit."

I teared up over that because of all the insults from people in the past, and then to hear such a compliment was really making up for the unkind things people have said or done to me. He had seen Jesus in me and that I don't take credit for it. My point being is that ever since the impartation of apostleship was given to me, I felt a shift in the spiritual sense that my prayers were now getting answered quickly, and this guest speaker ministering in the prophetic confirmed that in me. Praise God for impartations.

The previous day, my author friend said she wanted me to read her journal. She said normally she does not allow people to read her journal but that she would let me read what she wrote the night before. She wrote about a vision she had of herself in heaven and that she was sitting on the stairs in heaven. She saw the child who was aborted but prayed and asked the Lord if He would reveal to her if it was a boy or girl. He let her know that the child is her grandson, and she sat and visited with him a little while. He was seven years old with brown hair parted on the side.

I was very touched by reading this miracle vision. I had lost a child to miscarriage two months before I was pregnant with Sofia, my youngest child. When I read this story, I asked the Lord if he would do the same for me. I asked if He would show me if it were a son or daughter that I lost. Also, I asked if I could please see what that child looked like now.

I thought that my answer to that prayer would be awhile, but the next night while we were worshiping before the service started there was a young Hispanic man who was playing guitar very proudly. I could see the spirit of worship all about him. As he glanced in my direction, I felt a pulling sensation toward him. It felt as though the Lord was trying to impress something upon. I asked the Lord if He was trying to tell me something. He responded, "Didn't you ask me something so important to you yesterday?"

I said, "Yes, Lord."

He responded, "What do you see?"

"I see a young man." Just then I gasped and asked, "Are you saying that this is what my miscarried baby looks like?"

He said, "Yes, my love, and what else do you see?"

I said, "He's playing a guitar."

The Lord God answered my prayer just like that and showed me what my son looks like and that in heaven he is playing a guitar worshiping the same Father God that I worship. The Lord said, "Now that you know, you can name him."

When I got home from that conference, I explained the whole story to Sofia. I took a picture of that boy, showed it to Sofia, and she was deeply touched as well. Now we both are trying to agree on a name for my son, her brother, who is in heaven and whom we shall see someday. I will give him a big hug and call him by his name.

Since then, while I was driving to work and thinking lots about my handsome respectful son in heaven, I asked God if he is with my parents and if my parents know that he is their grandson? Father God responded, "Yes and yes." Just then, I saw a vision of him standing there with my parents, and then I saw my dog Vixie, who died around the same time as my mother. I saw my son smiling and petting the dog. What a vision! I shall always remember it well.

The conference ended, and the women I connected with decided to meet up at their hotel room. I had checked out of my hotel early, so I could ride with them in the morning to the airport and not have to pay extra for transportation. We were just filled to the fullest with the anointing, and we wanted to just touch bases with one another and get each other's contact information. We met up in one of the rooms, and we just kept sharing the goodness of God and sharing each other's stories of what God was doing in our lives.

We began praying for one another and getting so blessed that we did not want to leave each other. They asked me what I was believing God for, and I shared that I had a problem with my neck. A few of them prayed, but I had the same sensation of pain when I turned my head in any direction; however, I could hear cymbals. Even after everyone's prayers were done, the pain did not go away, and I felt a little embarrassed by one woman who persisted. She took me aside and asked me what happened in the past regarding the trauma to my neck and hearing; she received a word of knowledge that my hearing was affected.

I explained about my past with domestic violence, that my ex-husband had tried to choke me to death. As far as the hearing, I would hear my parents fighting as a young child, and it scared me so much that I would often cover my ears so I would not hear the yelling. The loud sounds would send me into a panic attack with sudden shaking and trembling all over and hyperventilating. She said, "That's it," and then we began saying the forgiveness prayer together, one for my parents and then another for my ex-husband. When we finished, I felt the healing come. The sensation on the back of my neck was gone, and my hearing opened. I suddenly could hear much better. I was so happy. I could not believe at first. I wondered, *Can this be true?*

The morning came, and we left to the airport. One of my new friends, who was sitting beside me, had a very soft voice so I used to have to ask her to repeat what she said, but this time, I could clearly hear her speak every word! The taxi driver had his music playing, and he was sharing how he became a Christian. Previously, I would have had to ask him to turn his music down so I could hear him, but not this time. I could hear him perfectly. When I got home, my daughter could tell that my hearing had improved because I didn't have to ask her to speak up. When I got back to work, the volume on my Bluetooth was a little too high, so I had to turn it down. Glory to God!

In running my race in life, I know that I am climbing higher with the knowledge that I am deeply loved by my Father God. I also know that my earthly father did his best to take care of me and love me in the way he knew how. When I was able to understand that love, I knew my true value and no longer listened to the deceit of the enemy. Having a higher calling, I do understand my past and the impact, but I now look forward to the future, even in these golden years. Through true forgiveness, I've experienced physical healing in my body. Everything I have endured was for a purpose because when I am used to minister to those suffering, I can truly say that I know their pain. I'm a survivor and a true soldier in God's army doing His work, helping believers know that they are fully equipped to run their race and finish strong.

SELF-REFLECTION

- Are you satisfied with your relationship with God today?
- What are key scriptures you can go to that highlight the Father's love for you?
- Do you believe you are forgiven for your sins?
- Is there anyone you need to forgive who is causing resentment and bitterness in your life?

CHAPTER NINE
EMPTY NESTER

CLOSER AND STRONGER TO GOD

Now that I'm through the ordination process and back home to my routine of work and rest, I feel a sense of accomplishment. But more than that, I feel such a closeness with my Father God, and the plan He has for me is clearly laid out in front of me. There is a reality that all this time my earthly father, John Madrenas Miramontez, was in heaven petitioning God the Father on my behalf with Jesus, along with my mother, Adrianna Miramontez. My dad knows that I will be working in a ministry preaching the Word of God and ministering to people of all denominations and cultures about running life's race but having a great start by thrusting forth on hinds' feet. I see both my parents nodding their heads in agreement and pride in me their youngest daughter–Nettypie. Just as they were in the stands rooting for me in my all-girls track meet, they are beaming with joy from the balconies above with the same enthusiasm along with angelic hosts.

We have what it takes to jolt forward with all our might because we were created in God's image, fully capable of enduring all of life's challenges. What I know in my heart is connecting with what I know in my mind, so I can now rest in the Father's love and experience true inner peace. Walking in God's plan fits like a glove because I am doing His work in daily situations where He brings people in my path who need prayer and healing. My cup runs over like a babbling brook. When there is something funny, I have a deep belly laugh that is true joy. No longer will I hide in the shelter of humor from anything that is gone awry because He has redeemed me from family disfunction, and I have been set free.

I now have full understanding of who God is. No longer am I the child inside, pulling at my mother's cotton flowered dress in Catholic Mass, asking if the priest up front was God. Nor do I investigate the faces of one of the pristine statues placed dutifully behind the priest and ask if that is God. The right time would come for that nine-year-old girl, sitting in Mass in reverence and hearing the voice of God Himself, calling me by name and answering my questions. It was then that I would learn who God is. He is my Prince of Peace, He is everywhere, and He lives in me. I'm a daughter of the King, of a royal priesthood, so who else would be my prince but Jesus? Because I know my God as my Prince of Peace, being an empty-nester is not as bad as I had imagined. There is peace with this part of my life.

MY CHILDREN AND CHILDREN'S CHILDREN

With my youngest daughter, Sofia, now living with her older sister, Kristy, and my granddaughter Mariyah, I have entered this different stage of life, and it is much more acceptable to me. I now live alone in my two-bedroom apartment in a not-so-favorable location, but I am going through this for good reason. Maybe I shall fully appreciate Joseph's story from the pit to the palace.

It has given me the much-needed solitude to write his book. I work full time as a housekeeper still in a clinical setting for a Native-American community that treats me well, and it is probably the best job I've ever had. The benefits are great, and this is where God has me; perhaps I will retire from here.

Sofia is attending school in Oregon, and it seems to be the ideal situation for her success. I had no idea that this was the answer for her and get caught up with how far she had fallen behind from us relocating several times. My next step is to get started with an agency that will help me get my credit score up and then get a lender. I am attempting to get into a Habitat for Humanity home.

Since I've gotten older, parenting my children has taken a different form. Parenting adult children is a change because there are healthy boundaries in motion. I do not give advice unless it asked of me. I do not criticize or judge when something goes wrong. When a situation arises, which may be often, it prompts me to ask them if I may pray for them. I have never been turned away. We have been amazed at God's answers to our prayers that have come through in praying by text or phone calls. Bringing my adult children to the cross and laying them at the feet of Jesus has given me great peace. I can rest knowing that Father God has them under His covering. I always pray for them to have godly wisdom, insight, and revelation.

Holidays are much easier these days because our dinners are at my oldest daughter Melissa's home. I have accepted this new normal as well. She lets me relax and watch a movie as she cooks and cleans. I do manage to make the homemade pies though. I usually get to see my grandson Peyton who comes home from college. Grandkids are the best part of life, and I would love to have more.

RETURNING TO MY FIRST LOVE OF WRITING

There have been many times when I have suffered through bouts of depression not knowing that I could have been walking in victory much sooner. Like Maya Angelou once said, "Do the best you can until you know better. Then when you know better, do better"[6] I know when I use the giftings that my Father God made in me, I am happy and content. When I make time every week to do some artwork and do my writing, I feel like I have fed my soul. I journal in what I call a book of remembrance, where I write about how God answers prayers. God is always answering prayers, and we forget to thank Him.

As I come to the end of this book, I want to remember and honor my great grandfather, Andrew Seltice, on my mother's side. He was the last chief of the Coeur d'Alene tribe. They now run the tribe with elected council members. He was a gifted writer and orator. He handwrote the book, The *Saga of the Coeur d'Alene Indians*. Year ago, my aunt Barce took his manuscripts and had his book published, and I remember my mother being so proud and excited. She made sure that each one of her nine children got a copy. Now I treasure my copy, and I like to read her personal inscription in her cursive writing to me.

Today as I write, I feel his gift of writing and speaking alive and well in me, passed down from generation to generation, and I am humbled. I appreciate his legacy. If he had not written it all down, I would have never known the stories that took place before me with the prophetic gift in our ancestors and their prestigious names.

CREATIVITY

Even though it has been many years since I have done any artwork, it is not too late to begin again. I am inspired through the lyrics of the Daystar Singers and their song, "You Can Begin Again." No longer will I listen to the negative voices telling me it is too late or too much time has gone by and you won't be any good at it anymore. I just decided that the time is now, so I started to get back into painting again. I had just made another hand drum at our employee retreat, and I wanted to paint something on it, so I started there.

Then I started to paint on canvas, which was a little more challenging. I am learning to see colors and variations. It is great to take notice of God's creations and how beautifully perfect they are in all the different aspects that I can capture on canvas. I have a lot of catching up to do since I have not painted in such a long time. I now have the time to do this. This time I now have is for me. I will use it well. Sometimes I just do some sketches or doodle with colored pencils in coloring books. Other times, I paint oil or acrylic on canvas. There are always more ideas coming to mind, and I am loving it.

MINISTRY WORK

Now that I know that ministry work is in my near future, there are preparations that I am doing as I am learning about them. I am fascinated with the tools I can use share what God has done in my life using social media. I have stepped out of my comfort zone and produced my first video, thanks to help from Charity Bradshaw and her author coaching. I'm excited to see what is next.

I look forward to speaking engagements and ministering to the hurting and lost through my book. Writing this book has been a catalyst for so much more happening for me through ministry work. When situations and circumstances take place that are prompted through the hand of God, then everything comes to pass at a moment's notice. It is all in God's timing, which is always perfect.

NEW LIFE

In this new season in my life, there is so much possibility, and it feels so right. There are new dreams to dream and new goals to reach. I stay connected with the group of women I met through Joan Hunter Ministries. We were ordained together, and we do a weekly phone conference to uplift and pray for one another. We will be getting together for future events.

I would like to do a children's book and a devotional. As I make more art pieces, I want to get into beading necklaces and earrings to sell. I will be connecting with other vendors and learn any secrets to success from other artists.

> *"The Lord bless thee, and keep thee: The Lord make his face shine upon thee, and be gracious unto thee: The Lord lift up his countenance upon thee, and give thee peace." (Numbers 6:24–26, KJV)*

May He grant you success as you run your race in life, and may you have deep knowledge and understanding that your anointing is for your race and no other. May you run with great zeal and tenacity.

May each person reading this book receive a special anointing to be able to finish this race called life and finish strong receiving the victor's crown of life.

In Jesus' name, we seal this blessing. Amen.

ABOUT THE AUTHOR

Annette Miramontez is from the Pacific Northwest and is a devout prayer warrior, speaker, and artist who is ordained under the Joan Hunter Ministries. She was born into her specific family to pass the baton of faith to future generations.

She reaches out to those in need of prayer on social media or whomever crosses her path in those God-orchestrated moments. Her ministry, Heaven Sent Ministries, includes speaking engagements and book signings. She desires to see God heal, deliver, and set many people free across the United States and abroad.

Annette is an enrolled member of the Coeur d'Alene tribe of Idaho from her mother's side as well a product of her grandfather's endeavors for a better life in her Mexican American heritage from her father's side. She is a mother of six children and two grandchildren.

annettemiramontez.com

heavensent.com

ENDNOTES

1 Kowrach, Edward J. and Thomas E. Connelly. 1988. *The Saga of the Coeur d'Alene Indians. An Account of the Chief Joseph Seltice*. Fairfield, WA: Ye Gallion Press.

2 *Harper's Bazaar*, "21 of Maya Angelou's Best Quotes to Inspire," May 22, 2017, https://www.harpersbazaar.com/culture/features/a9874244/best-maya-angelou-quotes/.

3 https://www.lexico.com/en/definition/endurance Accessed January 10, 2022.

4 Natalie Grant and Steven Malcolm, "Even Louder," written by Joseph Prielozny et al., *The Second City* CD, Curb Records, Nashville, TN, April 26, 2019.

5 *Our Daily Bread*, August 23 daily reading, "No Fishing Allowed," by Amy Boucher Pye. The book referenced is *Tramp for the Lord* by Corrie ten Boom, (New York: Jove Books, 1978), https://odb.org/US/2020/08/23/no-fishing-allowed, Accessed November 15, 2021.

6 *Harper's Bazaar*, "21 of Maya Angelou's Best Quotes to Inspire," May 22, 2017, https://www.harpersbazaar.com/culture/features/a9874244/best-maya-angelou-quotes/.

Made in the USA
Middletown, DE
14 February 2022

61119506R00086